THE PEN AND THE SWORD

THE PEN AND THE SWORD

CONVERSATIONS WITH EDWARD SAID

DAVID BARSAMIAN
INTRODUCTIONS BY EQBAL AHMAD
AND NUBAR HOVSEPIAN

Haymarket Books
Chicago, Illinois

This edition published by Haymarket Books in 2010
P.O. Box 180165
Chicago, IL 60618
www.haymarketbooks.org
info@haymarketbooks.org

First published by Common Courage Press in 1994
© Edward W. Said and David Barsamian, 1994
Introduction to the 1994 edition © Eqbal Ahmad, 1994
Introduction to the 2010 edition © Nubar Hovsepian, 2010

Trade distribution through Consortium Book Sales, www.cbsd.com

This book was published with the generous support of the Wallace Global Fund.

Cover design by Eric Ruder.

ISBN-13: 978-1-931859-95-0

Printed in the United States.

Library of Congress CIP Data is available.

CONTENTS

ACKNOWLEDGMENTS

In 1979 I was producing "Ganges to the Nile," a weekly program on Eastern music on KGNU in Boulder. Edward Said's *Orientalism* inspired me to contextualize the program within a political, cultural, and historical framework. Even though I have moved on from "Ganges," Edward Said continues to inform my work. It wasn't until 1987 that I met him at a talk he had given at a school on New York's Eastside. A few days later we did our first interview. I remember his asking expectantly, "Do you have some good questions?" Since then both the questions and answers have continued. Some of the interviews in this collection were broadcast nationally and internationally on Alternative Radio. They were all recorded in person in New York except the last one, which was done by phone.

Thanks to H. Aram Veeser and Zaineb Istrabadi for their encouragement, advice, and suggestions, and to Sandy Adler for transcribing the tapes.

I am very appreciative of Eqbal Ahmad for writing the introduction.

I feel a kinship with Edward Said rooted perhaps in my own background in which the themes of exile and dispossession were so prominent. My gratitude to him is fused with much affection and respect.

David Barsamian
Boulder, Colorado
June 1994

INTRODUCTION TO THE 1994 EDITION

At the outset one may ask: why this set of interviews with a writer as prolific and widely known as Edward Said? Most of his books are regularly assigned in hundreds of college courses throughout the United States and Europe. *Orientalism* is virtually a classic; its argument is learnt by osmosis and it is cited even by those who have not read it. Said's views are also conveyed to millions of people through his articles in popular publications and his frequent interventions on radio and television. What use then is this slim volume of interviews?

One answer is that this book reveals more than any previous work the person behind the name. Most of Edward Said's writings are scholarly and analytical. The mind is all there but not the man. Some of his books, including *Orientalism, The Question of Palestine*, and *Covering Islam* also contain polemic, which give us glimpses of the experiences and feelings that contributed to his formation as a critic of great originality and oppositional outlook. A smaller body of narratives—*After the Last Sky*; "The

Mind of Winter," an essay on exile in *Harper's* magazine (September 1984); a haunting account, also in *Harper's* (December 1992), of his brief return to Palestine; and a BBC documentary *The Edward Said Story*—provide biographical information but barely reveal the linkages between the writer and his life. David Barsamian's sympathetic questioning helps span the breach. These interviews are unique for the connections they uncover between the man and his ideas.

Edward Said is among those rare persons in whose life there is coincidence of ideals and reality, a meeting of abstract principle and individual behavior. Since the publication of *Orientalism* (1978), the word "courageous" has been used often to describe his writings. In real life, his courage is palpable and a source of inspiration and comfort to family and friends. I am reminded of an incident some years ago. Three friends dined in Beirut with Faiz Ahmed Faiz, the Pakistani poet who had taken, from the U.S.-supported tyranny of Mohammed Zia ul-Haq, a refuge of sorts in war-torn Lebanon. Said was fully engaged as Faiz recited a poem "Lullaby for a Palestinian Child." Just then a violent firefight started nearby; the waiters scurried inside leaving us the only diners in the courtyard. Instinctively, I stopped translating from Faiz's Urdu into English, and looked inquiringly at Nubar Hovsepian, who knew Beirut and its warriors well. "Go on," urged Said as if nothing unusual was happening. We went on.

"When he is absorbed, he doesn't care," Mariam Said once told me. Gradually, I understood also that his absorption is willed, and his courage is sustained by a lasting sense of intellectual purpose and moral outlook. At times his life was threatened by violent groups so seriously that the FBI would warn him to be careful. He was careful as best he could be but he never heeded friendly or expert advice to take a vacation, avoid public engagements, or curtail his advocacy for the liberation of Palestine. Even when those threats to his life coincided with the actuality of assassination, as when Isam Sartawi was murdered in Paris and Abu Jihad in Tunis, Edward lived normally. When Barsamian asks how he dealt with the death threats, he replies: "Not to think about it too much...if you dwell on any problem of that sort, then the worst is accomplished by incapacitating you.... It's harder on other people than it is on yourself.... I think the main thing is to just keep going and remember that what you do and say means much more than whether you are safe or not."

The threats did not stop after the PLO joined the negotiations in Madrid, nor after Yasser Arafat signed an agreement with Israel. Merely, the sources of menace have changed. These are scoundrel times in the Arab world where augmented foreign interests coincide with the collapse of sovereign will and internal corruption. In an environment of generalized capitulation, patriots are perceived as dangerous by governments that rule by coercion rather than consent. "I'm on half a dozen death lists in the Middle East," Said tells Barsamian. Meanwhile, another enemy stalks him, and he confronts it without losing a moment of his purposeful life. "[A] lot of people are concerned about your health. They ask me about you. What can you tell them?" David Barsamian asks at the end of these conversations. "It's a holding pattern," he replies: "I have a chronic disease, leukemia. It has its bad moments.... I try not to think about the future too much.... I've got a lot to say and write, I feel, and I just want to go on doing that."

"Amazing!" my wife had exclaimed as Edward returned enthusiastically to work and extensive travels, days after leukemia had been diagnosed. He corrected the galleys of *Culture and Imperialism.* When it was published he traveled widely to publicize it in the United States and Europe, surprising his editors with his enormous energy, power of concentration, wit, and humor. The BBC documentary on him was also filmed at the time. We met in London to record a segment of it; during the three days we were there, I battled jet lag while Edward kept his usual eighteen-hour schedule. Soon thereafter, he was preparing the Reith Lectures for the BBC while teaching, lecturing, going regularly to the opera, and partying with family and friends.

During all this time Edward was engaged in the losing struggle to prevent Yasser Arafat's slide to surrender. It began in October 1991 when the PLO chairman joined the Madrid peace conference under U.S.-sponsored and Israeli-dictated terms that were humiliating and harmful to Palestinian interests. In effect, the PLO surrendered in Madrid its claim to represent the Palestinian people, and also the right of occupied Jerusalem's inhabitants to be represented; and it agreed to the exclusion of two and a half million Palestinians in exile. Edward was among the few Arab intellectuals who understood that Arafat had entered a process not of peace but capitulation. He warned PLO leaders—including Arafat—weekly, sometimes daily, that they were embarked on a defeatist course.

One morning in January 1993, we drank coffee in his Riverside apartment when the phone rang. The intense conversation in Arabic lasted about forty minutes. Edward returned, exasperated, beads of perspiration on his forehead, and said: "They will end up guarding the world's largest prison: Gaza." In the fall, I thought of this incident in Islamabad as I watched on television that very sad ceremony at the White House and recoiled, as Edward seems to have done, at Arafat's repeated "thank yous" to Clinton. "Thanking the U.S. for what?" he asks, and recalls the brutalities and violence that surrounded this historic accord.

Said had been an early advocate of peace with Israel. Had Yasser Arafat responded to the proposal he brought to Beirut in the fall of 1978 and again in March 1979—he reveals the details here for the first time—a reasonable Palestinian-Israeli settlement might have been possible. Said considers the recent PLO-Israeli accord a "capitulation" by Arafat, and offers reasons to justify this consideration. I should let others and history judge. I note here only those aspects of his objection that relate to his intellectual formation. They involve his preoccupation with memory, with the narrative of the oppressed, and with the commitment to never let a dominant myth or viewpoint become history without its counterpoint. Equally important to his work are his deep sense of personal and collective loss, and his quest of positive and universal alternatives to sectarian ideologies, structures, and claims. Throughout his work these themes are strung together on strings that connect knowledge and power and establish the links between culture and imperialism. He makes these connections always in ways that open a more interesting and humane alternative—a counterpoint, a culture of resistance, the promise of a non-sectarian, secular liberation.

The PLO-Israeli negotiations began in the fall of 1992 in Boston before they found a neutral sponsor in Oslo. Israel has a history of escalating violence during negotiations and ceasefires. So, from October 1992 to September 1993 was among the "worst periods of oppression on the West Bank." Many people died, mostly kids under eighteen. Four hundred fifteen Palestinians were expelled from their homes in open violation of international law and abandoned to the bitter winter on Lebanon's border. People in the occupied territories spent most of this time under curfew, cut off from the outside world, and even from each other since the occupiers controlled the roads and enforced the curfews. Israel invaded Lebanon again, this time with the expressed objective of creating several hundred thousand refugees. None of these grim facts merited a mention at the ceremony in the Rose Garden. Imperialism and power-driven myths were on display instead, and there was no hint of resistance. The Palestinians' narrative was overwhelmed by Israeli claims, this time with the complicity of Palestine's proclaimed representative.

Said was invited to the White House, did not go, and watched the "tawdry" affair on TV: Clinton was "like a Roman emperor bringing two vassal kings to his imperial court and making them shake hands in front of him. Then there was the fashion show parade of star personalities…and most distressing of all were the speeches in which the Israeli prime minister Rabin gave the Palestinian speech, full of anguish, Hamlet's anxiety and uncertainty, the loss, the sacrifice, and so on…. Arafat's speech was in fact written by businessmen and was a businessman's speech, with all the flair of a rental agreement." It appeared obscene that just when South Africa was breaking free, there was all this hoopla over creating a bantustan in Palestine; but Said's pain was obviously different and deeper.

A bad accord is bad enough. Palestinians have battled and somehow survived many disasters. They may survive this one too. But Arafat's failure to produce a counterpoint to Rabin's narrative and offer a witness to his people's extraordinary pain touched something deep in Said's emotional and intellectual being. In the "general political economy of memory and recollections that exists in public culture in the West, there is no room for the Palestinian experience of loss," he tells Barsamian while recounting the haunting experience of visiting Israel in 1992, for the first time since his people were forced out of there. Occasionally, memory overwhelms him; he could not bear to enter his home in Jerusalem, now occupied by Christian Zionists, and standing outside, merely identified to his children the room in which he was born.

A person with so profound a sense of loss should be bitter, as many Palestinians are. Said is not, perhaps because of his abiding commitment to exploring alternatives. This quest led him to seek reconciliation with Israel. After the 1967 war, he was among the first Palestinians to argue that Arab refusal to "recognize Israel's existence" was a sterile posture. He consistently referred to Israel as Israel, dismissing as very silly the ritual term "Zionist entity." The Jews are there to stay, and the Palestinians are there to stay, he said repeatedly, and no amount of violence, deportations, expulsions, and pretensions can change this reality. He believed that the only alternative to permanent warfare and violence was politics— project a vision of Palestine attractive to Arabs and Jews alike, and pursue it with a certain "discipline of detail." Year after year, since 1970, I heard him argue with PLO leaders that politics must be the primary instrument of liberation that flows from sustained work in civil society both at home and abroad, that the conflict shall eventually have to be settled at the negotiating table, and that the PLO was woefully short on political analyses and diplomatic skills. They gave him respectful hearings. That is all.

True to his belief, Edward was the first Palestinian intellectual I
know who met with Israelis and American Zionists. Among them
was Simha Flapan, the Mapam leader who later wrote with great
courage and scholarship on the Palestinian experience of Zionism. Among them also were some well-known American Jewish
leaders; some of them later became supporters of Peace Now.
There is barely an Israeli peace activist who did not meet Edward
Said. He was also the first prominent Arab intellectual to openly
criticize Palestinian terrorism as a wrong and counterproductive
liberation strategy. Occasionally, he felt alone then, as he does
now, only to discover that others were with him.

The rhetoric during the 1970s and 1980s of Zionist leaders fa-
vored direct Israeli-Palestinian negotiations, peace on the basis
of equality, and an end to occupation in return for Arab acknowledgment of Israel's right to exist. Their stated agenda was
not significantly different from what Said advocated. Why then
did he become such a bête noire of the Zionist establishment? One
answer is ironic: his very peaceability and accurate estimation of
Zionism were perceived as serious threats by the Zionist establishment. But what irked them most was his determined telling of the
Palestinian story, his constant interventions with a "counterpoint,"
his quest of alternatives to sectarian nationalism.

All nationalist movements spawn myths about themselves. Zionism has the distinction also of creating a large body of myths
about Palestine and Palestinians: Palestine was a land without a
people for a people without a land: a desert made to bloom by
the labor of Zionist pioneers; a wasteland sparsely inhabited by
Bedouins: a backward Ottoman satrapy that awaited the trans-
forming hand of European Immigrants; a Jewish land from

"time immemorial," and so on. As for Palestinians: they did not exist: the Arabs fled Palestine in 1948 because Radio Cairo asked them to flee; the so-called Palestinians came to Palestine from Syria, attracted by the economic miracle of Jewish Aliyas, etc. The myths run into the hundreds.

Edward Said was unique among Arab scholars for comprehending that those myths are products of a need greater than propaganda. He understood their central importance to the epistemology of Zionism. Palestinians have the misfortune of being oppressed by a rare adversary, a people who themselves have suffered long and deeply from persecution. "The uniqueness of our position is that we are the victims of the victims," he tells Barsamian. The tormentors of European Jews had always been motivated by sectarian ideas and sentiments. Yet, this people dispossessed another under the banner of an exclusionary ideology that sought to systematically build a Jewish homeland where there was for millennia a Palestinian homeland. Therein lay the most fundamental contradiction of Western Jewry in relation to Zionism, Israel, and the Palestinians. Blaming the victims, devaluing their humanity, demonizing them, provided the easiest escape from this contradiction.

With his interest and insights into the strategic deployment and uses of culture, he understood that in their ensemble those myths were integral to the epistemology of Zionism, a mechanism for the legitimation of the Jewish state and also of the Zionist movement's inhumanity to a kindred people. Edward Said is given to "writing back," a habit most disconcerting to those who would rather not confront the truth. He "wrote back" to Zionism and its supporters from the moment his consciousness was focused on the question of Palestine. His very first essay on this subject, "Portrait of an Arab" (reprinted in *The Arab-Israeli Conflict of June 1967: An Arab Perspective*), appeared soon after the 1967 war. With passion and textual acuity he exposed the malice and racialism with which the media had caricatured Arabs during and after the war. In a tour de force he linked the widely prevalent anti-Arab bias in the West to anti-Semitism, which, ironically, the Jews themselves were now eagerly mobilizing against the Arabs. I recall him portraying the Palestinian as a shadow of the Jew, a shadow that won't disappear except in a human embrace. Thereafter, he kept "writing back," and those are among the most brilliant of his writings from the literary and political point of view. I should mention specially "Zionism from the Standpoint of Its Victims" (in *The Question of Palestine*), "Exodus: A Canaanite Reading" (in *Blaming the Victims*), and *After the Last Sky*. I should note that since he first began to deposit the Palestinian experience of loss in what he calls "the memory bank of the world," a group of Israeli revisionist historians have appeared to expose more myths, and the truth comes increasingly to light.

Any Jew reading Edward Said on Zionism and Palestine will experience one of two emotions—remorse or anger. Tragically, the angry ones outnumber the remorseful. He informs Barsamian that when he reported in *Harper's* on his visit to Israel to "the sites of personal catastrophe for me"—both the magazine and the author received many "angry, appalling letters.... One person who claimed to be a psychiatrist, for example, prescribed a psychiatric hospital for me. Others accused me of lying.... I found that very disheartening." This posture of militant intolerance is not confined to obscure letter writers. The determination to deny the Palestinians a voice and the right to self-expression is widespread. Each one of us can tell a story of suppression. Said recalls how Joseph Papp, the New York producer and director who was widely respected for his commitment to liberal causes, canceled a show by Hakawati, a West Bank theater group. Disheartening indeed!

But whenever he encounters remorse, an acknowledgment of injustice done, Said is touched; his hopes for reconciliation are renewed. He recalls in these interviews two such incidents, one an encounter with an anonymous Israeli taxi driver, another with Matti Peled, a retired Israeli general and war hero. When Peled visited New York, Said invited him to lunch. As Peled described his hectic life as a peace activist, Said asked: "Matti, why do you do this?" Peled said: "In one word, remorse. I feel remorse." Said says that "it had such a powerful effect on me that even when I think on it I choke up.... It filled me with admiration and regard for him." The taxi driver, who must have recognized Edward, said "I'm an Israeli." "Fine. I am a Palestinian," Edward replied. "I didn't serve," said the Israeli. When he got off and the taxi sped away, Said was saddened: "It struck me that in a certain sense it was a moment lost to the future."

Not exactly, because Said made sure that neither encounter enters oblivion. When two men, apart from each other, broke the barriers of denial and silence they connected with the third man and created, as Said argues in another of these interviews, a genuine alternative, a parity between two people, and therefore the possibility for the oppressor and the oppressed to "belong to the same history." It is thus that memory, remorse, and redemption are linked. This recent Israeli-Palestinian accord negates

that dialectic and commits the Palestinians to a state of permanent inequality and domination.

A constant in Said's work is his opposition to sectarian ideologies, attitudes, and practices. The compelling motive in his critical work is an abhorrence of racialist, exclusionary, and separatist
values. This was a primary basis of his critique of Orientalism. It
remained an abiding theme in *Culture and Imperialism*. This re-
coiling from the sectarian outlook shapes his harsh indictment of
contemporary Arab states and their brand of nationalism, and
also his anxiety over what is happening in Palestinian politics.
During the decades I have known him, he has remained deeply
committed to Palestinian liberation without ever losing sight of
the "limitations of nationalism...a self-centered vision of the
world that infects us all." In these interviews he returns to this
theme repeatedly. We read, for example, "when national consciousness becomes an end in itself, and ethnic particularity or
racial particularity or some largely invented national essence...
becomes the program of a civilization or culture or political
party, you know it's the end of the human community."

Dedication to universalism in politics, culture, and aesthetics
serves for Said as a counterpoint to sectarian options. It is a question, he once said, of whether you enter history with open arms or
a tight fist. The roots of his universalist beliefs lie, I think, in Arab
civilization; in his upbringing in Jerusalem and Cairo; in the Western tradition of Enlightenment; and in the Palestinian experience.
In Arab history, his interest has been focused largely on culture.
This necessarily entails a special attention to those periods—for
example, the eighth to eleventh centuries of Islam, the thirteenth
to fifteenth centuries in North Africa and Spain, the nineteenth

and much of the twentieth century in the Fertile Crescent and Egypt—when the intellectual and aesthetic environment was specially lively, ecumenical, and universalistic. Here is how Said describes the world in which he grew up:

> All the schools I went to as a boy were full of people of different races. It was completely natural for me to be in school with Armenians, Muslims, Italians, Jews, and Greeks because that was the Levant and that was the way we grew up. The new divisiveness and ethnocentrism that we now find is of relatively new vintage and completely foreign to me. And I hate it.

His critique of Israel's exclusionary ideology, structures, and practices grates on Israel's supporters, but it is consistent with this outlook. The Law of Return grants a Russian, French, Nigerian Jew the automatic right to settle in Palestine while Edward Said is deprived of his natural right to belong where he was born and his ancestors had lived for centuries until Israel's creation. The Arab inhabitants of Israel are denied the rights of citizenship equal to those of their Jewish compatriots. Said once wrote that even the kibbutz system, a socialist institution, is a form of apartheid. The struggle for Palestine has meaning for him only in this context. The "essence of our conflict," he tells Barsamian, lies in the notion that "Palestine belongs only as Israel to the Jewish people and not to all the others who happen to be there."

Said's outlook owes a great deal to the Palestinian experience. It is through suffering, the experience of dispossession, that he achieves universal consciousness, and that leads him to Nelson Mandela in Johannesburg or C. L. R. James in London. In this there is a parallel between his life and ideals and those of many

European and American Jews. Jewish humanism drew on Jewish aesthetics and mysticism, and on the ideas of Enlightenment. But it was also defined by a history of suffering and persecution. Jewish attraction to universal values and ideologies, liberal and socialist, was a function, in part at least, of their reaction against sectarian enemies. Unless Israel changes as South Africa has changed, history may regard it a tragedy that a people so formed became committed to an ideology of difference and discrimination. Said worries that his people may also choose a similar path.

Joseph Conrad inevitably appears in these interviews, as do Jane Austen, T. S. Eliot, and Albert Camus. I have often wondered about Edward's attachment to Conrad. His first book was on him, and references to Conrad abound in nearly all his works. Conrad was an exile like Said, one who crossed the boundaries of culture and mastered another's language, as Said has done. This he does not say. But he speaks of an intellectual debt to Conrad, telling Barsamian that Conrad was "one of the most extraordinary witnesses...to the role of culture in imperialism," to the centrality of ideas—of service, sacrifice, racial superiority, and redemption—in the making and maintenance of empire. More than any other novelist Conrad understood "how empire infected not just the people who were subjugated by it but the people who served it." Conrad understood imperialism, its inner force, and its dark side. He had "the outsider's sense that Europe was doomed in a certain sense to repeat this cycle of foreign adventure, corruption, and decline." But he saw it as inevitable.

It was left to the African, Caribbean, and Asian writer to imagine the alternative and start writing back. Edward Said is foremost among those who pushed this quest forward beyond nationalism and postcolonial statehood, crossing boundaries to interpret the world and the text "based on counterpoint" as he would say, "many voices producing a history."

Eqbal Ahmad
Islamabad, Pakistan
June 1994

EDWARD W. SAID: THE CONSCIOUS PARIAH[1]

In 1994 Eqbal Ahmad penned the introduction for the first edition of this book. He passed away in Pakistan on May 11, 1999. Eqbal's friends and family celebrated his life at a memorial service held in New York. Two of Eqbal's dear friends and coconspirators for justice, Edward W. Said and Ibrahim Abu-Lughod, spoke eloquently about Eqbal's legacy. Two years later, Ibrahim passed away in Ramallah, Palestine. Edward felt very lonely, he missed his dear friends. Edward dedicated his book *Orientalism* to "Janet and Ibrahim," and *Culture and Imperialism* was in turn dedicated to Eqbal. Death separated him from his friends, but even before death, Eqbal and Ibrahim had migrated "home," the first to Pakistan and the second to Palestine, while Edward remained in exile.

Edward wrote moving eulogies paying tribute to his friends and acknowledging their role in educating him about politics. He describes Eqbal's life as "an epic and poetic one, full of wanderings, border crossings, and an almost instinctive attraction to

liberation movements, movements of the oppressed and the per-
secuted…whether they lived in the great metropolitan centers of
Europe and America, or in the refugee camps, besieged cities,
and bombed or disadvantaged villages in Bosnia, Chechnya,
south Lebanon, Vietnam, Iraq, Iran and, of course the Indian
subcontinent." Eqbal "managed unostentatiously to preserve his
native Muslim tradition without succumbing either to frozen ex-
clusivism or to the jealousy that has often gone with it. Humanity and genuine secularism in this blood-drenched old century of
ours had no finer champion."[2]

In an essay titled "My Guru," Edward remembers his departed
friend Ibrahim. He met Ibrahim in 1954, and it was Ibrahim who
introduced him to Eqbal in 1970, "the other comrade-in-arms
whose untimely death has left me so diminished."[3] Edward credits
Ibrahim with having introduced him to the subject and experience of Palestine. It was also Ibrahim who in 1974 introduced him
to Shafiq al-Hout, a member of the PLO delegation to the United
Nations General Assembly, and the Palestinian poet Mahmoud
Darwish, and in the process lured him to identify publicly with
the PLO and the question of Palestine. Ibrahim lived in Beirut
during the Israeli invasion of Lebanon in 1982. Edward notes that
"Beirut was perhaps the most important experience for Ibrahim
than any before or after." This experience taught him "that one can
always press on, even though failure looms. That was the real
Ibrahim: the man who understood that the only thing is to press
on, remaining optimistic and loyal to one's comrades (and making the most of one's sense of humour, however macabre").[4] Edward notes that for their final years both Eqbal and Ibrahim
returned to their countries of origin. He quickly adds, "But they

didn't actually go back home." Here Edward echoes a central message of his memoir, *Out of Place*.[5]

At two-year intervals, Eqbal then Ibrahim died. Then Edward died, two years later, on September 25, 2003. Over a period of six years, we lost rare human beings who together represent the best of what public intellectuals should be. None of these men belong to the past alone. As Edward put it, "these men stood for energy, mobility, and risk."

Edward was eulogized by friends, family members, former students, admirers, and even some enemies. Edward's funeral was almost a stately affair. It filled the pews of the Riverside Church in New York, the city that was home away from home. One of the most moving moments of the funeral was a musical tribute preformed by Edward's friend and collaborator in the founding of the West-Eastern Divan Orchestra—Daniel Barenboim. He played J. S. Bach's "Prelude in E-flat" from Book I of the *Well-Tempered Clavier*, with tears rolling down his face, but in silence. This was perhaps the first time that one of Barenboim's performances was met with appropriate silence and not applause.

Since Edward's death the situation in Palestine has gone from bad to worse. The Palestine movement has imploded, and Israel continues to unleash its wrath against the Palestinians as evidenced by its war on Gaza, as well as the continued expropriation of Palestinian lands, resources, and dignity. Such conditions can lead to despair. But Edward suggests an alternative path, which serves as a conclusion to his "My Guru": "In the unfolding story of Palestine, Ibrahim, I believe, will remain the model of what it is to have been dedicated to an idea—not as something to bow down to, but to live, and to re-examine constantly." He asks us not to copy what Ibrahim and other comrades-in-arms did, but to live their experience anew to enable the possibility of critical reflection and revision in the present and future.

Edward introduced me to David Barsamian knowing that we could become kindred spirits in our capacity as the non-Armenian Armenians. Edward was right. Through five interviews, conducted between 1987 and 1994, David Barsamian displays his expansive knowledge and engagement with Edward's work. He engages Said in dialogues that connect and weave together Said's ideas on culture, imperialism, Orientalism, exile, and Palestine. Barsamian's questions display his worldliness, which in turn allows Said to connect his humanism to his political engagements.

Edward has long been recognized as one of the world's leading cultural critics. Michael Sprinker edited one of the first books on Said.[6] Sprinker noted that Said "incarnates the very ideal of the cosmopolitan intellectual that remains so central to the humanities' self-image today."[7] Said contributed to focal debates in a vast number of social scientific disciplines, including history, sociology, anthropology, and area studies—particularly the Middle East. Said's *Orientalism*[8] and his subsequent books have created new fields of study, including postcolonial studies. With each book (about thirty in total, many of them translated into more than thirty-five languages) and his constant and sustained interventions as a public intellectual, Edward remained committed to a liberating humanism. In the dual role as a prolific scholar/intellectual and a public intellectual, Edward insisted that boundaries and barriers must be transgressed. He believed that intellectuals in modern society should speak "truth to power." Like Julien Benda, Edward believed that the intellectual must insist on truth and justice, and give utterance not to mere fashion and passing fads but to real ideas and values, which cannot be articulated from inside a position of power.[9]

Edward was a nuanced and complex man. He is one of the few modern thinkers, along with Noam Chomsky, Raymond Williams, and Michel Foucault, to have critically interrogated the modernist project. At once, he can identify the spectacular successes of modernity and its disastrous failures. This is precisely what he set out to accomplish through both his literary work and his cultural criticism. Edward did not so much defend Islam or the Arabs as attack the reified notions of Orient and Occident. His primary concern was to delineate the sources of Western knowledge about non-Western societies. Like a mirror, *Orientalism* reflects Western power and its imperial appetite. To rescue the production of knowledge from colonial and imperial constraints, Edward used a humanistic critique that "is centered on the agency of human individuality and subjective intuition, rather than on received ideas and approved authority." For Edward, the real task of the intellectual "is to advance human freedom and knowledge."[10]

At a celebration of the twenty-fifth anniversary of the publication of *Orientalism*, Gyan Prakash dubbed his Princeton colleague Bernard Lewis the "embedded intellectual," one who serves power. In contrast, Edward was the quintessential oppositional intellectual. Edward's conception of the intellectual both echoes and expands Antonio Gramsci's agenda for the "organic intellectual." He or she must uphold broad moral interests, especially in defense of the deprived and oppressed of society. Edward insisted that the intellectual must never shy away from criticism because of loyalty to nation. In *Representations of the*

Intellectual, he implores native intellectuals to resist the tempta-
tion to "narcotize the critical sense, or reduce its imperatives,
which are always to go beyond survival to questions of political
liberation, to critiques of the leadership, to presenting alternatives that are too often marginalized or pushed aside as irrelevant
to the main battle at hand."[11] He exhorts the modern intellectual
to resist the lures of power and specialization. The independent
intellectual must universalize and give greater scope to the crisis
confronting any nation at any given time by associating that experience with "the suffering of others."[12] It is precisely these
moral concerns that Said invokes to probe issues pertaining to
Palestine and the Middle East.

Edward's *The Question of Palestine* should be read as an essay in
reconciliation. He did not deny Jewish claims to Palestine; rather,
he would say that "their claims always entail Palestinian dispossession." Because he remained a proud and unapologetic Palestinian,
ardent Zionists and neoconservatives launched puerile and vindic-
tive attacks against him. Their attacks failed to offer the slightest
hint of an inclusive and humanistic model of coexistence. In sharp
contrast, Edward's friendship and musical collaboration with
Daniel Barenboim in founding the West-Eastern Divan Orchestra
offers a model of hope predicated on the building of community
by crossing cultural boundaries. He articulated this inclusive vision
many times. In 1983, he addressed a memo to the Palestinian National Congress in which he said that the world must see that the
"Palestinian idea is an idea of living together, of respect for others,
of mutual recognition between Palestinian and Israeli."[13]

It is noteworthy that *The Question of Palestine* has never been
published in Arabic.[14] Arab nationalists and some radical Palestini-

ans accused him of frittering away Palestinian rights by making "unwarranted concessions to Zionism." According to them, Said's key failure is in defining the conflict as one "between two peoples," instead of a class struggle against Zionism and imperialism. The Popular Front for the Liberation of Palestine (PFLP) said Said's failings were a function of his "bourgeois humanistic approach," which makes him distrustful of "armed struggle," instead favoring a political solution.[15]

But it is precisely the idea of mutual recognition between two peoples that first led Edward to advocate a two-state solution, as early as 1980, despite criticism from, among others, Yasser Arafat's circle. But in 1988 the Palestine National Council adopted the two-state formula. Edward was ahead of the curve, though his positions did not remain static.

After the 1982 Israeli invasion of Lebanon and its devastating human consequences, Edward teamed up with Jean Mohr, a Swiss photographer, to produce *After the Last Sky: Palestinian Lives*, a moving portrait of Palestinians.[16] Two years later he wrote an article titled "Permission to Narrate."[17] He wanted to rescue Palestinians from being mere objects of dismissive representation. Instead, he gave his people and their culture an active voice.

After the first intifada and the lead-up to the first Gulf War in 1991, Edward was concerned that Palestinian rights might be frittered away. In this connection, in September 1991, he asked me to organize a meeting he wanted to convene in London. He invited a select number of Palestinians from the occupied territories and others from the vast diaspora to think together about how the Palestinian national movement should respond to the Madrid peace conference to be held that October. The attendees urged the

PLO to participate in the Madrid conference, but with certain provisos. The Palestinian leadership embraced the call to participate, and eschewed the provisos.

Just before this meeting, Edward had visited South Africa. On the plane ride from South Africa to London he sat next to the African National Congress (ANC) ambassador to Great Britain. Edward invited the ambassador to address the London gathering. Not all who were present appreciated Edward's reasoning, but they listened. Edward wanted to convey a simple message. The Palestinian national movement was at a critical crossroads. It had no military option, but it still needed to conduct a wise but militant struggle. Such a struggle would require the mobilization not only of Palestinians, but of international public opinion. Toward this end, the ANC representative informed us about the internationally organized anti-apartheid campaign. The purpose of the campaign was to create an international moral climate to force a political showdown with the apartheid system. The message was clear. PLO participation in Madrid should be accompanied by the launching of the Palestinian equivalent of the anti-apartheid campaign: Israeli Occupation Must End. For diplomacy to yield positive results, more politics and grassroots mobilization, on the home front and internationally, were needed.

During a break before the London meeting's last session, Edward came to my hotel room to call his wife, Mariam, in New York. What he learned during that conversation was life-altering. His doctor wanted to see him upon his return to New York. He suspected that Edward might have leukemia. Edward asked me not to share this devastating news with anyone. He had scant time to digest it himself before presiding over the last session. Everyone noticed the change in his demeanor. He seemed preoccupied, a bit resigned. Everyone was perplexed.

Edward was indeed shaken and seemed withdrawn, but his resignation did not last long. This was the first and last time he allowed himself that luxury. From that moment on, he decided to live. He fought pessimism, opting to continue his mission of speaking truth to power—but with a sense of intense urgency. His body was subjected to ordinary and experimental treatments. After each grueling hospital visit, he wondered aloud if he could go through another. But, as the next treatment approached, he would say, "Do I really have another choice?" Thus despite his chronic illness, he wanted to "press on with the tasks at hand. I've got a lot to say and write, and I just want to go on doing that."[18] This is precisely what he did until his last day. His courage in the face of personal adversity inspired people all over the world to struggle for justice in Palestine and elsewhere.

I wrote the first chapter of the Sprinker volume on Said, titled "Connections with Palestine."[19] It is perhaps this connection, more than others, that put Said in the public limelight in the United States and in the West. In his eulogy of Edward, the Palestinian poet laureate Mahmoud Darwish observed, "Edward placed Palestine in the world's heart, and the world in the heart of Palestine."[20] But Palestine (place, people, idea) is, to state the obvious, controversial, particularly in the United States. For years Said was seen in the U.S. media to be "Arafat's man," or the voice of Palestine. But from the signing of the 1993 "Oslo Agreement" between Israel and the PLO, Said unleashed a systemic critique of the PLO leadership, through articles in various international outlets including *Al-Hayat*, *Al-Ahram*, the *Nation*, the *London Review of*

Books, and many other outlets. Many of these articles were collected in at least four books.[21] He considered that the PLO, in ac-
quiescing to a bad "peace," had now joined the other side and was
talking about the obliteration of the past. He argued that the idea
of a collective memory was rapidly becoming disallowed even by
Palestinians. This was unacceptable to him. Thus, he called upon
Arafat to resign.

Why did Said turn against Arafat? And why were Arafat's former enemies (Israelis and Americans) annoyed with Edward? *The
Politics of Dispossession* (1994) is a useful volume that answers
these questions in essays written over a quarter century. Here Edward introduced, discussed, advocated, and criticized the Palestinian movement. Though some of the essays might be dated
today, they nevertheless provide an important chronicle of the
adversity confronting the modern Palestinian movement since its
reactivation after the 1967 war. It is a history full of setbacks, as
evidenced by the wars and crises that the PLO and the Palestinian
people have had to endure. During the period of adversity, Said
supported the Palestinian leadership's quest for independence
and statehood. Since 1991, when the PLO leadership acquiesced
to U.S. conditions for participation in an international peace conference, Said faulted this leadership for succumbing to unacceptable conditions, and in fact viewed them as the equivalent of a
Vichy government that has lost sight of its people's fundamental
objective: self-determination for the West Bank, Gaza, and all
Palestinians. Instead, the goal of self-determination has been replaced with limited self-rule for Palestinians.

Peace and Its Discontents (1993) can be viewed as a companion
volume to *The Politics of Dispossession.* In this collection of essays,

Edward presents the reader with a "dissenting record of what took place for almost two years, from the 'historic handshake' on the White House lawn in 1993 until, roughly speaking, its second anniversary."[22] Unlike most observers, Said maintains that the "Oslo Peace Process" is deeply flawed because it is ultimately a "peace" without any semblance of justice. Said insists that from the secret negotiations in Oslo to the present, Arabs have capitulated unnecessarily, and Israel has in fact "achieved all of its tactical and strategic objectives at the expense of nearly every proclaimed principle of Arab and Palestinian nationalism and struggle."[23]

> For the first time in our history, our leadership has simply given up on self-determination, Jerusalem, and the refugees, allowing them to become part of an undetermined set of "final status negotiations." For the first time in our recent past, we accepted the division of our people—whose unity we had fought for as a national movement since 1948—into residents of the Occupied Territories and all the others, who happen today to constitute over 55 percent of the Palestinian population; they exist in another, lesser category not covered by the peace process. For the first time in the twentieth century, an anticolonial liberation movement had not only discarded its own considerable achievements but made an agreement to cooperate with a military occupation before the occupation had ended, and before the government of Israel had admitted that it was in effect a government of military occupation. (To this day Israel has refused to concede that it is an occupying power.)[24]

Edward refused an invitation from the White House to attend the 1993 signing ceremony because he viewed it as a day of mourning for all Palestinians. Tony Judt, in his introduction to Edward's collected essays *From Oslo to Iraq* (2008), commends Said for his courage. Judt was one of many who initially welcomed the Oslo process, but he notes that "in retrospect it is difficult to deny that he got it right and we got it wrong."[25]

Let me be candid. I too was less than enthusiastic about the prospects of the Oslo peace process. Even before the White House ceremony of 1993, I expressed my doubts in an article titled: "Will Arafat become the Israelis' Enforcer?"[26] The question mark in the title represented my only concession to optimism. Since then I have not only followed the unfolding events, but I have seen their impact through numerous visits to occupied Palestine. Put simply, Edward was on the mark. Instead of peace, Palestinians are subjected to expulsions and closures, daily expropriations of land and their resources. Their lands are punctuated by increasing and expanding settlements, bypass roads, and the "wall," which Palestinians experience as an apartheid wall. All of this, for Edward, would not be possible without the United States, whose unconditional support of Israel enables it to perpetually dispossess the Palestinian people.

Edward was furious at the Palestinian Authority (PA) during Arafat's reign and after. He lambasted the PLO and the PA for their corruption and ineptitude. He criticized the Arab regimes on the same counts and more. He charged that the PA willingly accepted a new role—native policemen whose task is to quell Palestinian resistance to Israeli occupation. Edward would have been even more furious to witness how the PA has evolved under Mahmoud Abbas's leadership. His forces are trained by U.S. advisors to help defeat their compatriots from Hamas. He might have used the title of one of his articles, "Suicidal Ignorance,"[27] to lament the futility of fighting between Fatah and Hamas. Instead of leading Palestinians in difficult times, the Palestinian national movement imploded in Gaza in August 2007. Edward would be calling for the reconstitution of the PLO to represent the entirety of the Palestinian people, including those in the diaspora.

In the last years of his life, Edward's ideas evolved further. He went back to his humanistic principle that insists on inclusion rather than exclusion. He reasoned that historic Palestine and historic Israel are ostensibly lost causes. The security and prosperity of Israelis and Palestinians are inseparable, hence to remain prisoners of exclusive victim narrative can only lead to further human tragedy and loss of life. Instead he wanted to dislodge the sterile discourse by moving it in a different direction. He expressed support for a binational state, one that could usher reconciliation based on a discourse of inclusion rather than domination. He asked us to think of how Palestinians and Israelis can live with rather than against each other.[28] By turning his attention to alternative formulations, he joined the company of earlier thinkers who in the nineteenth and twentieth centuries tried to envisage an alternative to Zionism.

Gabriel Piterberg dubbed Bernard Lazare and later Hannah Arendt as "conscious pariahs" who represented the makings of a progressive alternative to Zionism by advocating binationalism. He adds, "the perspective of the conscious pariah is morally and politically viable even—perhaps specially today."[29] But, Edward, unlike other proponents of this idea, abstained from proposing a political agenda of how to implement this vision or define its final shape. At heart he remains a democratic humanist who insists that we must incorporate, emancipate, and enlighten. In the last few lines of his *Humanism and Democratic Criticism* (2004), Edward offers the following words:

I conclude with the thought that the intellectual's provisional home is the domain of an exigent, resistant, intransigent art into which, alas, one can neither retreat nor search for solutions. But only in that precarious exilic realm can one truly grasp the difficulty of what cannot be grasped and then go forth to try anyway.[30]

Edward's oeuvre is vast and indeed more books by him were published posthumously than most scholars publish in a lifetime.[31] He weaved in and out of interconnected domains—literature, music, politics, and history—insisting that to understand the world we must search for a balance between dissonance, consonance, and discord. In his memoir, *Out of Place*, he saw himself through this complicated prism. He is not a coherent single person, but many different things. In effect, his life affirmed and celebrated his and the world's multiple differences.

The philosopher of education Maxine Greene, author of *The Dialectic of Freedom*, shows how, in learning through the arts, the world is disclosed in "incomplete profiles."[32] Speaking to a conference in South Africa in February 2001 in an address titled "The Book, Critical Performance and the Future of Education," Edward built on Greene's observation with the following words:

> Surely a great lesson of the last hundred years is that none of the great or small systems, whether imperial, ideological, racial, religious or socio-economic, is adequate to the world's complexity, which cannot be herded neatly under one or other totalizing rubric. Such systems are false gods that routinely end up lapsing into barbarism and tyranny. Hence the alternative notion, that the world is incomplete, in the process of becoming, a magnificent series of fragments, certainly uncontainable by reductive schemes, nationalist or otherwise. Greene is right to say that, as Vico had suggested in the

mid-eighteenth century, the world presents itself to the learning mind in incomplete profiles.[33]

And here, too, emerges another of Edward's central imperatives as a humanist scholar: the importance of seeking alternatives to dominant ways of thinking, a value that animated every word he ever wrote.

Nubar Hovsepian
March 14, 2009

1. I am indebted to Gabriel Piterberg for this idea. In his new book, *The Returns of Zionism* (New York: Verso, 2008), Piterberg's dedication reads: "In Memory of Edward W. Said (1935–2003), the conscious pariah par excellence."
2. Edward W. Said, "A True Struggle, a Good Man," *Al-Ahram Weekly*, May 9, 1999.
3. Edward W. Said, "My Guru," *London Review of Books*, December 13, 2001.
4. Ibid.
5. Edward W. Said, *Out of Place: A Memoir* (New York: Alfred K. Knopf, 1999).
6. Michael Sprinker, ed., *Edward Said: A Critical Reader* (Cambridge, MA: Blackwell Publishers, 1992).
7. Ibid., 1.
8. Edward W. Said, *Orientalism* (New York: Pantheon Books, 1978). The text remains widely used today not only in literary theory, but anthropology, sociology, history, politics, and women's studies.
9. See Julien Benda, *La Trahison des Clercs* (Paris: Editions Bernard Grasset, 1927).
10. Edward W. Said, *Representations of the Intellectual* (New York: Pantheon, 1994), 17.
11. Ibid., 41.
12. Ibid., 44.
13. Previously unpublished address by Edward W. Said, used with permission of Mariam Said and the Wylie Agency.

14. A request from one publisher asked for more than eighty changes. Previously unpublished letter, used with permission.
15. "The Question of Palestine According to Edward Said," *PFLP Bulletin*, no. 47, February 1981.
16. Edward W. Said, *After the Last Sky: Palestinian Lives* (New York: Pantheon, 1985).
17. Edward W. Said, "Permission to Narrate," *London Review of Books*, February 16–29, 1984.
18. As told to me by Edward Said.
19. Nubar Hovsepian, "Connections with Palestine," in Sprinker, *Said: A Critical Reader*.
20. Mahmoud Darwish, "Edward Said: A Contrapuntal Reading," translated by Mona Anis, Al-Ahram Weekly Online, September 30–October 6, 2004, http://weekly.ahram.org.eg/2004/710/cu4.htm.
21. Said's numerous books on the subject include: *Peace and Its Discontents* (1993); *The Politics of Dispossession: The Struggle for Palestinian Self-Determination, 1969–1994* (1994); *The End of the Peace Process: Oslo and After* (2000); *From Oslo to Iraq and the Road Map* (2004, published posthumously). All of these books are published by Pantheon Books.
22. Edward W. Said, *Peace and Its Discontents* (New York: Vintage Books, 1996), x.
23. Ibid., xxv.
24. Ibid., xxix.
25. Tony Judt, Introduction in Said, *From Oslo to Iraq*, xii.
26. Nubar Hovsepian, "Will Arafat Become the Israelis' Enforcer?" *Newsday*, September 5, 1993.
27. Edward W. Said, "Suicidal Ignorance," Al-Ahram Weekly Online, November 15–21, 2001.
28. Edward W. Said, "The One-State Solution," *New York Times Magazine*, January 10, 1999.
29. Piterberg, *Returns of Zionism*, xvi.
30. Edward W. Said, *Humanism and Democratic Criticism* (New York: Columbia University Press, 2004), 144.
31. These books include: *Humanism and Democratic Criticism*; *From Oslo to Iraq*; *Music at the Limits* (Columbia University Press, 2008); *On Late Style: Music and Literature Against the Grain* (New York: Vintage Books, 2008).
32. Maxine Greene, *The Dialectic of Freedom* (New York: Teachers College Press, 1988).
33. Previously unpublished talk by Edward W. Said, used with permission.

THE POLITICS AND CULTURE
OF PALESTINIAN EXILE

MARCH 18, 1987

David Barsamian: Talk about the qualities of being a question, for that suggests something not known and uncertain.

Edward Said: And it also suggests something uncertain as to its existence. People ask the question of Palestine as if to say: Does Palestine exist, or doesn't it? I think that's the most important aspect of, as you say, "being a question." People tend to want to eliminate Palestine from existence, although, of course, it's had an existence in the past and there are lots of people—4.5 million of them today—who call themselves "Palestinians." But the name "Palestine" is a highly provocative one in the minds of a lot of people. Unfortunately, even in the minds of Palestinians themselves, it has caused many of us a slight tremor in our awareness whenever we pronounce the name because it seems to be a rather threatening and challenging name. It's not a neutral noun, by any means.

What might be some cultural responses in answer to this question? We've seen the political responses.

In many ways the cultural responses are much more interesting and more varied. There was a period in the immediate decade after 1948 when Palestinians were essentially silent and unknown, that is to say, they were so shattered by the loss and the destruction of their society that they essentially went into a state of almost blankness. Beginning in the late 1950s there was a kind of resurgence, the first resurgence, I would say, of Palestinian national consciousness. It appears in a group of writers and journalists and activists in Israel, the group called El Ard, which included poets and novelists and, as I said, journalists. They didn't last very long, that is to say, their enterprise, which was a printing house and a newspaper, was shut down by the Israelis a couple of years later. But under the influence of Nasserism, a lot of Palestinians began to articulate their national consciousness, in novels and poetry and plays and above all in essays, in writing of a journalistic and discursive kind. But especially after the 1967 war, the Palestinian voice began to represent and symbolize, culturally speaking, the voice of truth in an Arab world which had obviously been defeated, by its own hypocrisy and by Israeli arms. So that the Palestinian exile and resistance poet, represented by people like Mahmoud Darwish, Ghassan Kanafani, and others, achieved a kind of international status by virtue of the rather stunning and quite powerful directness of their voices and the emergence of what in effect was a new language, which included not only the disenfranchised Palestinian male but also women writers and writers out of sectors of the population that had historically not been articulate: workers, teachers, and people of that sort.

So you suggest that the efforts to characterize the Palestinians as terrorists, nomads, refugees, hijackers, have been unsuccessful?

I think in the long run they have been unsuccessful. They have achieved a kind of identification in the minds of some people for a short period of time as Palestinians with all these negative qualities. But all you need is an experience like the invasion of Lebanon in 1982 by Israel and immediately all of these clichés collapse and you get a new sense, a disturbing sense, of the Israeli reality, although it's very, very difficult. The police action of discursive limits of what's allowed and what isn't is very strong. Some Palestinian stories, some experiences penetrate this web of negative characterizations that you've referred to, and the clichés are dispersed.

I won't say that it's been unsuccessful. Of course these efforts are very successful to the extent that Palestinians are in fact recognized as dehumanized beings, terrorists, and so forth. Yet, for Palestinians themselves these labels have no meaning, and for more people that are willing to listen to the story, they have no meaning either. It's amazing to us, those of us who speak and write and talk, that around in this country people are interested in hearing the story because it's a story to which they haven't been exposed.

Connected with that might be the notion that interest in Palestine seems to have some extra-dimensional quality. It's not a simple up-and-down political question.

No, because Palestine itself is a very unusual and exceptional place. I suppose all places are exceptional, but Palestine is simply more exceptional than others. It has a Biblical resonance, obviously, a very powerful one. It has a historical resonance. It's been in continuous existence, producing demons and saints and gods and so on, for millennia. And partly because of its geographical location. It is an intersecting point between major not only religions but cultures. The cultures of East and West intersect there, Hellenic, Greek, Armenian, Syrian, Levantine, broadly speaking, and the European, Christian, African, Phoenician—it's a fantastic conjuncture. In this respect Palestine itself is always something that wriggles free of one confining label or another. And this is very important: insofar as Palestinians represent the plural, the multicommunal aspect of Palestine. Their struggle is staked not only on exclusivity and the monopoly of what Palestine means, but rather the intersection of many communities and cultures within Palestine, the Palestinians partake in the richness of Palestine. What we have fought is a people and ideology saying that Palestine belongs only as Israel to the Jewish people, and not to all the others who have to be there in a subsidiary position. That's really the essence of our conflict with Zionism.

In *Orientalism* you discuss the role of intellectuals, scholars, and experts who served British and French imperial designs and power in the Middle East. They provided the framework, justification, and rationale for conquest and domination. Is there a comparable class at work today on the Palestinian question?

I think so, certainly in the United States and Israel. There is, and has been since the very beginning of the state of Israel in 1948, a class of Orientalists or "Arabists," as they are called, whose job has been to work with the government to pacify, dominate, understand, and control the native Palestinian Arab population. You see their ranks in the occupation government of the West Bank and Gaza, where Orientalists, people who are specialists in Islamic history and culture, work with the military occupation forces as advisors. Menachem Milson, who was the administrator of the West Bank up until 1983, is in fact a professor of Arabic literature. So you have a direct continuity between classical Orientalism and Western imperialism in the Islamic world and elsewhere, and Israeli Orientalism and imperialism in the occupied territories.

In the United States you have a similar phenomenon. You have a whole cadre now of so-called experts, I call them Orientalists, whose job it is to provide through their expertise in the Islamic and Arab world both the media and the government with what I would call hostile attention to the Arab world. For example, there was a symposium on terrorism recently published by a major publisher here. It was edited by the Israeli ambassador to the United Nations. Three of the articles were written by noted Orientalists who tried to show that there was a particularly urgent coincidence between Islam and terrorism. This kind of thing goes on.

There's a whole group of these people, numbering thirty or forty, who are trundled out whenever there's a crisis, a hostage crisis, a hijacking, a massacre of some sort or another, to demonstrate the necessary connection between Islam, Arab culture, and the Arab character, as it's sometimes referred to, or the Islamic character, and random violence. To my mind, the great misfortune is that these Orientalists whose role is to understand, to interpret the culture of Islam and the Arabs, and it's a culture from which they earn their living, in fact have no sympathy with it. They deal with it from an adversarial and oppositional position. In that respect they are functionaries and hostages, in effect, of

U.S. government policy, which is deeply hostile to Arab nationalism and Islamic culture.

That's been true, I think, ever since the two came into contact.
This situation does not seem to be changing, although there are a
number of younger people now who are beginning to combat this
particular phenomenon in America. But the fact is that if you look at
the material, you'll see that the people I'm referring to, these Orientalists, whose attention and interest and scholarly expertise in Islam
is harnessed to these imperial purposes by the United States, have access to the major media, that is to say, they can write in the *New York
Times*, the *New Republic*, *Commentary*, etc., right down the line there
are these blanket condemnations of the Arabs in articles and representations of them by this hostile group with very little to deter
them. People of my persuasion, or Chomsky's or others, have no access, or at least have very little access, and nowhere near the access
that these other people do who can avail themselves of the resources
of the *New York Times* or CBS or PBS without any trouble at all.

**You've said on the issue of Palestine that there is much more pluralism
of opinion in Israel than in the United States.**

That is a striking fact that anyone who knows anything about
Israel, Israeli or non-Israeli, Arab or non-Arab has remarked.
There is in this country a fantastic unanimity of opinion and even
an excess of zeal with regard to Israel amongst Jews and amongst
the organized Jewish community. The reasons for it seem to me to
be complex and obvious. There is a great deal of guilt at work
here, a great deal of fear and, above all, of ignorance. Israel is totally dependent upon the United States, so any criticism of Israel

is immediately interpreted by the supporters of Israel in this country as a threat to American support and therefore has to be snuffed out. There's very little awareness of the fundamental issues in Israel, that is to say, what are the issues facing each Israeli man, woman, and child as he or she has to conduct his life in the next ten years. Most American Jews know little about this and are not interested. For them Israel is simply a secular religion, a place to which money is sent. But the problems of having to live in a state of siege are not those that American Jews have to worry about and therefore they encourage it because it's the macho and militant and correct thing to do.

A lot of people participate in this, not only Jews. A lot of Zionists like George Will and William Buckley who have no urgent connection with Israel, may in fact be deeply antipathetic to Israel, nevertheless celebrate it. There has emerged during the Reagan years a large group of people, like Jeane Kirkpatrick, for example, and Alexander Haig, who regarded Israel as important to U.S. security and view it as a bulwark against communism, terrorism, etc. So Israel has assumed an unnatural importance which gets it a kind of blanket enthusiasm and munificence from the United States and people within the population that is quite unparalleled.

Unfortunately, this seems to be doing Israel nothing but harm in the long term, and perhaps even in the short term. But supporters of Israel are not interested in that.

I once asked an editor from National Public Radio about its extensive coverage of events in Israel. Every time someone sneezes, coughs, or burps, there's a story. I suggested to him that equally momentous events

of that nature go on in Algeria, Iraq, Syria, Egypt, and other Arab states and asked why weren't they being reported. The response was silence.

There's silence because obviously Israelis are like "us," whereas the others are not. They have different languages, they're different people, and therefore they're fundamentally less interesting and I suppose, although it's never said, less human than "we" are. That's certainly the case. One must also report this, as Robert Friedman has reported in a recent issue of *Mother Jones*, and Thomas Friedman of the *Times* has reported it also: there is a fantastic Israeli concentration on the U.S. media. By that I mean that there's a governmental attention to the media such that, according to Friedman of the *Times*, hundreds if not thousands of articles a year written in Israel by the Israeli information apparatus are passed into the U.S. media, newspapers, magazines, television, and radio. This kind of information effort results in unbelievably easygoing, uncritical coverage of Israel in the media. They're much, much less critical of anything that goes on in Israel.

That's one thing. The other thing is there is a kind of fear amongst journalists in this country that if they undertake to tell the truth about Israel and the Arab world, the retaliation against them would be very severe, that they would lose their jobs and so on. Paul Findley, in his book *They Dare to Speak Out*, talks about some of that. To be honest, I think a lot of that is exaggerated. I think the fear of retaliation is itself exaggerated because I don't think the means of retaliation are so great. So there is a kind of collective cowardice in the media.

A third point which has to be made is that most journalists, in my opinion, who now report on the Middle East are not journalists at all. They do no investigative work. They don't know the languages. They are in and out of a place if there's a crisis. They cover the canonical topics: terrorists, outrages, etc. For the rest, it's simply not covered and therefore deemed not interesting and therefore not there. There's no political awareness of what is going on in the Arab world. At this moment it's a seething cauldron of interesting and extraordinarily volatile currents and countercurrents and very little of this gets into the press because most journalists are simply lazy and incompetent.

The title of your book, *After the Last Sky*, is from a poem by Mahmoud Darwish. I'm interested that you quoted this particular poem. He says, "The earth is closing in on us, pushing us through the last passage." That suggests a double entendre of death and birth.

It was a poem that attracted my attention because it was written as a result of what happened in 1982, when Palestinians again, after 1948, had to leave a country which they had been established in, in this case Lebanon, in 1982 for the second time. Except that now we're dealing with a generation that was much more politicized, much more aware than the generation of 1948. So there was a sense of doom and yet, as you said, of rebirth, in other words, passing through the last sky and the last passage suggests that even though it may appear to be the last, there's still another avenue, there's another sky, there's another terrain on the other side. Exactly that double sense of it was what attracted me to it, as did the fact that I think for all Palestinians 1982 was the other great watershed in our experience, 1948 being the first. It seemed to me therefore necessary and important to take stock of the Palestinian situation after 1982.

Is it racist to expect more from Jews, from Israelis?

I'm not sure I understand what you mean.

Given the history of the Jews and the creation of the Israeli state, because of their historical experience with persecution and suffering and holocaust and death camps, should one feel that Israelis and Jews in general should be more sensitive, should be more compassionate? Is that racist?

No, I don't think it's racist. As a Palestinian I keep telling myself that if I were in a position one day to gain political restitution for all the sufferings of my people, I would, I think, be extraordinarily sensitive to the possibility that I might in the process be injuring another people. And one of the great puzzles to me, and it's a deep mystery, I must say, is how few, comparatively, Jews and Israelis I've met who, beyond embarrassment and discomfort when they meet a Palestinian, feel a sense of remorse and compassion for creatures who are going through in many respects what they went through. What's more disturbing, creatures who are going through what they went through but now because of them, because of what has been done by Israeli Jews to Palestinians, Palestinians are going through what Jews did before them. I'll never forget the almost shattering effect on me when Matti Peled, who once was a reserve general in the Israeli army, three or four years ago was in America and I invited him to Columbia. He's a man I respect and admire a great deal. He was describing his activities: he was running for the Knesset. Subsequent to that he was elected to the Knesset. We had lunch, and he was telling me about his activities. I turned to him and said, "Matti, why do you do this? It's extraordinary." He said, "In one word, remorse. I feel remorse." It had such a powerful effect on me that even when I think on it I choke up, that a man would say such a thing. It filled me with admiration and regard for him, and yet at the same time I keep wondering why so few people feel that remorse.

Stephen Daedalus in *Ulysses* says, "History is a nightmare from which I am trying to awake." What happens to the Palestinians when they awake from their national nightmare? Can you go a little bit into the future and envision a state? What would some of its textures and dimensions be?

I find it hard to do that in affirmative or positive terms. I couldn't give you a blueprint or a map of what a Palestinian state would be like at this point because I'm so concerned about some of the negative things that might be there against which I want to guard.

For example, I would hate for a Palestinian state to emerge out of a struggle of this sort and against enemies of this kind to simply be a carbon copy of other Arab states. I would hate for it to be like, say, Lebanon or Iraq. That's one thing. Secondly, I would hate for it to be a state that was riven with a minority consciousness, such as one finds today in Israel. I would hope that it would be a state that would have an easier sense of its own security and its own self-worth. That it wouldn't need to be in a state of siege. I think that's terribly important. And third, I would like it to be a state which would not have to become a security state in all the bad senses of that word, in which populations, groups, women, disadvantaged people, etc., would be discriminated against. Those things are more urgent to me to think about than the more positive aspects of whether the state would be a socialist state, capitalist state, and so forth. Those seem to me to be the real threats to any future Palestinian political survival.

You wrote *Question of Palestine* in the early 1980s.

Late 1970s, actually.

Are the Palestinians any closer to the realization of that goal of an independent state?

I would say in many ways, yes. I think most Palestinians now would not settle for anything less than that, whereas there was a time when most Palestinians felt that if they could just survive at all that would be enough. Politically I would say, probably no, given the situation in the Middle East, and here's the contradiction: there is a set of forces on the ground and in the air, so to speak, that militates so strongly against Palestinian self-determination at this moment that the prospects don't look in the immediate future very bright.

But I think we have to keep thinking about these things on two levels. One is the level of political will, which is stronger than before, I believe, because we've survived a great deal in the seven or eight years since I wrote the book. On the ground, in actuality, I think the challenge is greater. But I think it's the history of this people, and indeed of all people, that the more stiff the challenge, the more determined the struggle. I don't think people simply give up and lie down and die.

Is that quality of being beleaguered and under siege one of the reasons that perhaps has propelled the Palestinians in the Middle East, in the United States, and elsewhere to become quite a professional class?

There are many engineers, architects, professors, etc. I think that's been a natural consequence of the fact that a lot of us are itinerant. We've had to depend not on the accumulation of goods and capital but on the management of skills and resources like education, technical expertise, and intellectual capital. As a result, we are a wandering group in whose consciousness and awareness there is always the sense of being on the peripheries, slightly marginal to any society that one lives in. As a result, I think a lot of us have at the same time the feeling of delinquency, that we are delinquent but somehow privileged in some way, that we see things in a more acute way. There's a kind of gift of insight to a certain degree that is allowed Palestinians who can see the inequities, who can see the ironies of a situation, who know that laws are passed in many countries against them. We saw it here in this country where nine Palestinians are threatened with deportation because they purportedly bought magazines that claimed world communism as their goal. It's an irony that Swift would have enjoyed. It's this kind of sense that Palestinians have cultivated over time and I think Palestinian humor, which tends to be bitter and strong, nevertheless is very acute in its perceptions.

Again that Darwish couplet: "Where should we go after the last frontiers, where should the birds fly after the last sky?"

Yes, exactly. That's the sense of knowing that we seem to be at the very last frontier and the very last sky, that there's nothing after this, that we're doomed to perdition—and yet, we ask the question, "Where do we go from here?" We want to see another doctor. It's not enough just to be told that we're dead. We want to move on.

ORIENTALISM REVISITED

OCTOBER 8, 1991

David Barsamian: Welcome to the Land of Oz. I don't know if you've heard the recent press reports, but the Congress and the president have announced billions of dollars in loan guarantees to help build new homes and resettle the quarter of a million Palestinians who were living in Kuwait who have now been forced to emigrate to Jordan. I was wondering if you had heard that bulletin. Can you verify it?

Edward Said: No, I can't. I haven't heard it.

Do you find it rather capricious?

Yes. It's totally unthinkable, because it seems to me that the United States has in a rather purposeful way been waging war on Palestinian civilians for the last forty years. So any change of this sort strikes me as the tooth fairy, Oz, Pollyanna, Mr. Rogers, all rolled up into one.

Plus c'est change, ...

... plus c'est la meme chose.

Let's talk about the images and symbols of the early 1980s and compare them to the early 1990s. There was, for example, a *Newsweek* cover story in August 1990, shortly after the Iraqi invasion of Kuwait. They offered that in the Middle East "betrayal is the mother's milk of statesmen."

It's considered to be a society that is best exemplified by stories about a scorpion biting a camel crossing the river. The images that first come to mind are essentially nineteenth-century images. The whole idea of anomaly and anachronisms is best applied to current representations of the Middle East. The whole vocabulary of partly romantic, partly anti-romantic Orientalism is alive and well. It seems to have been taken over completely unchanged. You find it, for example, in the work of David Pryce-Jones, who wrote a book called *The Closed Circle: An Interpretation of the Arabs*, in which, as I recall, he admits he doesn't know Arabic and is not a scholar. But he ventures tremendously large generalizations about Arab culture as a shame culture, as a culture of violence, as a depraved and sensual and completely untrustworthy world. There was a review of his book by Conor Cruise O'Brien in a leading English newspaper shortly after the book came out. He says, here is the first man who tells the truth about the Arab world. It was picked up in a recent issue of *The Public Interest* and it's passed on. This is the way the Arabs are. And so we go. Nothing's changed.

Do you find that disappointing?

To me, it's what is expected from these people.

Where the disappointment and the sadness come in is that all the work that various Arab scholars and writers and interpreters of the Arab world, who are themselves combatants against the corruptions and cruelties of the various regimes—it's as if none of that makes any difference. The irony of it is that all these quite legitimate attacks on the political system in the Arab world, which is corrupt, rotting, putrefying, but no one of these Western experts, without any exception that I can think of, has ever identified or identified with a struggle within the Arab world against it. And there is a large opposition. For example, most of the best writers, journalists, artists, intellectuals, academicians in the Arab world are in the opposition now. Many of them can't write, can't speak, are under arrest, etc. No mention is made of that at all. The women's movement, the human rights movement, all of these are ongoing struggles in each country, although they're quite different in Egypt, say, or Jordan. But they're never mentioned. And above all, and the sign of this all, is that very little is made of the Palestinian struggle for freedom of expression, freedom to assemble, freedom to form political parties, etc. So you wonder what this is all about. The real sadness comes when you realize that all of this work has made no effect on them. They simply repeat what they're saying. To use the title of David Pryce-Jones's book, that's the "closed circle," not the Arab world, where there's a lot going on.

You've described the question of Palestine as being "inconvenient" for journalists and academics. I'd like you to explore that. These are not people who are running for office, not subject to political pressure such as lobbying. So why is it so inconvenient?

It's hard to say. I've really been up against it for at least thirty years in this country. They seem to be divided into three categories. There are the outright liars who say that there are no Palestinians, the Palestinian case is simply nonexistent. "They" left in 1948 because they were told to or they weren't really there to begin with, they came in from other Arab countries in 1946 in order to leave in 1948. There's a complete narrative behind it. In other words, "they" are miscellaneous people on the West Bank and Gaza. They're Arabs of Palestine but they're not Palestinians. That's the Likud line.

The second line is taken by the *bien pensants*.

They will rant and rave and go on and on at great length about South Africa, about liberal democracy in Poland, Czechoslovakia, and Hungary and China and Nicaragua. They're liberal democrats who then will say nothing about Palestine at all. They just won't say anything.

Then there are the third ones, who talk about Palestine but somehow make an exception for Israel. If you put to them the case and say, Well, there's all of this in addition to South Africa and Nicaragua and Vietnam and the Soviet Union and Tiananmen Square, there's Palestine, they'll say, Yes, there's Palestine, but Israel is not like the other side. So the question then becomes in the third category, Who is responsible if it's not Israel? If there isn't some monstrous injustice which Israel is perpetuating, with the support of American tax dollars and American liberals? Who is responsible? In the end they say it's the Palestinians' fault. They are responsible, and the other Arabs are responsible. But the whole thing for me is the inconvenience, is that there is unmistakably an Israeli Zionist burden of guilt which is monstrous. It bears only the most complicated and embarrassing relationship to the Holocaust and anti-Semitism, because you can't say all of this is a way for the survivors of the Holocaust to get reparations, or this is what is owed them by the Palestinians. You can't actually say that. But it's implied in a way, because if you don't say it, and don't try to defend that position, then in the end they are responsible. I'm not saying the Palestinians are innocent. But what we're talking about is the destruction of a society in 1948 and the deliberate, programmatic oppression of Palestinians ever since then, particularly in the twenty-four years since the occupation of the West Bank and Gaza in 1967, where there's an attack on the very identity—national, cultural, political, even the existential—of the Palestinians by systematically destroying us. So it's inconvenient, of course.

In your New School debate with Meron Benvenisti, the former Israeli deputy mayor of Jerusalem, and in other places as well, you insist that there be an Israeli acknowledgment of the "injustice," as you term it, that was committed against the Palestinians. Why is that so important?

Because what has killed us in the last thirty or forty years is the denial and the fact that they are not responsible. So we appear as if we are orphans, as if we have no origins, no narrative, no genealogy as a people. Our genealogy is only comprehensible, in my opinion, if Israeli action in it directly upon us is acknowledged. So what we're talking about is the acknowledgment of a history. That's number one. Number two, it at least brings us to parity with the Israelis, because we've acknowledged their existence. We've said to them, You are here. You've destroyed our society, you took our land, but we recognize your nationhood, in effect. We say to you that we want to live in peace with you in the following mode: we want a Palestinian state, self-determination for our people on the West

Bank and Gaza. You can have your state and self-determination for your people in pre-1967 Israel. They've never made that acknowledgment to us. They've never, as a nation—I'm not talking about individuals who say, Yes, yes, I have no trouble, but they never say it in public—when for the ten years before 1988, when Israelis would come and talk to me and say, We want acknowledgment from you. It would be fantastically useful if you accepted Resolution 242, if you recognized Israel. Then everything would change. Well, we did that, and nothing changed. It got worse. So I think for those two reasons we need to have the acknowledgment. The denial and the silence and in the end the indifference of American Jews in particular has been very, very bad for us.

Would that acknowledgment release the permission to narrate, as you call it?

I think it would make a great difference. Then we would belong to the same history. Our ability to tell our story will multiply by a factor of ten. I think it's important to understand that in the West there has been a systematic assault upon any attempt to narrate a Palestinian history by the Israelis. On the one hand, on the West Bank and Gaza, because people are so much in need of security, the Palestinians, to go from one day to the next, that the last thing they want to do is tell their story. They just want to survive. That is true of the Palestinians in Lebanon and elsewhere where they're under assault. The problem of survival is so great that you don't think in terms of narration, just in terms of getting through to the next day. Internationally, whenever a Palestinian effort to tell a story, to put in a dramatic and realizable way the interrupted story of Palestine and its connection to the story of Israel, it's systematically attacked. There has been no major feature run on Palestine. Whenever there has been a dramatic representation, for example, the Hakawati troupe tour, it's been criticized and stopped, most recently in 1988 when Joe Papp at the Public Theater canceled the contract. Whenever a film on television, a documentary appears, Joann Trout's *Days of Rage* on PBS, the examples can be multiplied, there's always the need to introduce a panel. At the Institute for Contemporary Art in Boston a few weeks ago there was a series of Palestinian documentary videos on recent events. They said they would stop it unless they had a panel with the "other side" represented. So we're always the other side of the other side. I think this has had the effect of making Palestinians incoherent, and every time you go and speak in public, as I do, you have to tell the story from the beginning. Second, it's made Palestinians incoherent and inhuman. You get the impression that you're not really talking about a people with a history. That is also a deliberate policy in the age of communications and the age of what Chomsky called "manufacturing consent." This is a very heavy burden on us, and we don't have the cadres. Most of our people don't live in the West. So it's a remarkably difficult task to remove that barrier.

What is the effect of Palestinians and other colonized people, for that matter, of having these histories buried by the hegemonic power? What would be a good metaphor to employ? Would you "dig up" that history? How could it be restored?

I think the most important thing about the history would not be to dig it up but to represent it, to speak it, to let it be without constant assaults on the speaker of that history, on the integrity of the messenger. I think the metaphor is realization in the dramatic sense. That's what I'm feeling more than anything else, that these are people who can be represented. The absence of a narrative, in my opinion, has made possible this totally *Gulliver's Travels* sort of condition, where at the projected peace talks the Palestinians cannot represent themselves. They can only represent themselves through the filter of Israeli denial and American complicity. So that conditions are attached. Not only that you can't be from East Jerusalem. You can't be from the West Bank and Gaza. You can't have had contact with the PLO. You can't be named by the PLO. You can't identify yourself as working at the instructions of the PLO, you can't even have seen somebody from the PLO. You can't be independent; you have to be part of the Jordanian delegation. You can't have a flag. You can't speak on your own. Those are conditions that are unheard of in international negotiations between peoples, and yet the Americans have accepted them because the Israelis have wanted them. So the idea is that the representativity of the Palestinian people is equivalent to their realization as human beings. So if you prevent their representation you don't have to realize them as human beings. That's why until this day Israelis of the Likud and Shamir in particular refer to Palestinians as "resident aliens or inhabitants." They don't have a history in Palestine. Shamir was asked on September 5, when he gave a talk commemorating the fiftieth anniversary of the founding of the Stern gang, he said, Terrorism is all right if it's for a just cause. Then a journalist asked him, What about Palestinian terrorism? He said, Their cause is not just. "They fight for a land that is not theirs," he said. So all of these issues are connected to history.

Also, one of the other operative myths in the mainstream media, in the United States, at least, is the one of the "missed opportunities." The Palestinians always have this knack for...

That's Abba Eban who started this. I was asked by a large American daily about the phrase, and I said it's a racist slander. Because we have of course missed opportunities. Every people does. But to identify us as the people who have always never missed an opportunity to miss an opportunity is really to say that we are characteristically inept, that it is in our genes, which is nonsense. We have taken more risks and leaped at more opportunities than any of the parties in the Middle East, certainly more than the Israelis, for that matter, who seem endlessly to be going to the right. So it's an unacceptable slander, based on racist presumptions.

Another component of that is Amos Oz, the Israeli novelist, complaining in *Liberácion* that "the Palestinians have always been on the wrong side: Hitler, Nasser, the Soviet Union, and Saddam."

Amos Oz is an interesting figure. He is part of this composite fair-haired acceptable Israeli figure who appears in the West, who speaks to the town hall in Hempstead and writers' groups in New York and has the agonized look of a man who's searching for a solution because, as people like him say, the occupation is bad for our soul, and look what it's doing to us. Never mind what it's doing to the Palestinians who are dying and being beaten up and tortured. But it's worse for us because our souls are at stake. Amos Oz, it seems to me, is a genuine Jekyll and Hyde. He will say phrases like, The occupation must end, we are against this domination of another people, at the same time that he presents opinions about the Palestinians that suggest that, as he says, They are the worst and most evil national movement in history. He has actually said that. There's a schizophrenic quality there where in order to maintain your credentials as a liberal in the West you have to attack the very people whom you're oppressing and blame it on them. It is exactly the replication of the arguments of anti-Semitism against Jews, classically, in the nineteenth and twentieth centuries. Exactly.

You're the leading spokesperson, whether you like it or not, in the United States for the Palestinian nationalist movement. Yet I sense in your work a certain ambivalence, mixed feelings about nationalism itself. For example, you've written, "Better our wanderings, I sometimes think, than the horrid, clanking shutters of their return, the open secular element and not the symmetry of redemption." Who are you talking about there?

I think mainly us. I think Palestinians are two things today. On the one hand, they're an independence movement, which is fueled by a kind of nationalist ideology, which is the form of resistance to oppression. In that sense, how could I not support it, because I'm part of it. But it has all the limitations of nationalism, essentially a Palestinian-centered vision of the world which infects us all. There's a certain kind of xenophobia connected to it, a chauvinism which is an inevitable part of any resistant nationalism. So that's one thing we are, and that to a certain degree but not completely responds to the pressures of Israeli oppression. The other thing that we are is an exile movement. I'm much more comfortable in that. Exiles, to a certain degree like Armenians after the 1920s, the ones who came to the West. You could call them cultural nationalists. But in our case, because the contact with the surrounding world, the Arab world, is still very great, it's not quite like that. But exile existence is really a full-time occupation now for more than half of our population. For the first time in our history, 55 percent of Palestinians live outside the land of historical Palestine. For these people, it seems to me we have to seek new modes of community and new modes of existence that are not based upon nostalgia, longing, dreams of return, which are real in all of us. We're not at the stage yet where we can deal with that completely. It's a very tragic experience. The result is that we waffle. Sometimes we're part of the independence movement. Sometimes we take our exile seriously. But the PLO, which represents all Palestinians whether we like it or not, like all nationalist movements has its orthodoxy, its official line, and I have sometimes been very uncomfortable with that, at the same time that, obviously, I support it. I think that gives you a range of the difficulties.

In *After the Last Sky* you quote from Yeats's "Leda and the Swan," "being so caught up, so mastered by the brute blood of the air, that she put on his knowledge with his power before the indifferent beak could let her drop." Who is Leda in this representation?

Palestinians, or the Palestinian conscience, which in a certain sense was raped by history the way Leda was raped by Zeus in the figure of the swan. My recollections of my early days in Palestine, my youth, the first twelve or thirteen years of my life before I left Palestine, maybe because of hindsight and retrospective nostalgia, suggest to me an attempt at being shielded. All of us were trying to shield ourselves from the obvious reality, that the place was being taken over and that there was going to be a fight between us and the settlers from Europe. Then we awakened in 1948 to the reality. My entire family was thrown out. It's interesting to talk about knowledge and power. Can you put on knowledge before the indifferent beak lets you drop from that power, the power of that source? It took me about thirty-five years to realize that, although I was aware of it, in a matter of months my whole family, on my mother's and my father's side, cousins, grandparents, uncles, aunts, etc., were all driven out of Palestine in 1948. Many of them, certainly those of the older generation, never recovered from the trauma. And in many of the younger generation you see the problems replicated: psychological, economic, and other problems get repeated.

I'm not clear about the "indifferent beak." I had a couple of readings on it. One, it's the imperial power itself, or the nationalist movements.

Both. I don't want to press the exact analogy with the poem too far, but you could say it is the experience of nationalism, and also that it is the experience with imperialism. These are the two that come to mind. But it's also the experience with your own history. In a certain sense, the intervention of the swan in her life is an entry into history. You are now part of the twentieth-century movement of empire, decolonization, liberation struggles, and resistance and the successful nationalism. We've had part of that. I must tell you that after I came back from South Africa I had a much healthier sense of how the Palestinian national movement, at least in the 1970s and the early 1980s, was really quite uniquely to the Arab world able to bring Palestinians into the twentieth-century experience of colonization, because of our connection with all of these movements. Mandela told me in Johannesburg in late May that "we will never desert the Palestinians, a) because it's a matter of principle, and b) because of your help for us." While the ANC was in its worst moments in the 1960s and 1970s, they were getting help from us, and from the Algerians and others. That was certainly true of SWAPO, of the Nicaraguans, the Vietnamese, the Iranians, all of these resistance movements were tremendously helped by the Palestinians, in Beirut usually. So that suggests an understanding of our own place in history, that we're not just an innocent, pastoral people, that we are part of this big movement. I think that's an important historical achievement, to know this. But as to where it's going to take us, that's another question.

But the Palestinian experience is so singular compared to other colonized people. For example, the Belgians come to the Congo. They seize it. They take out the diamonds. And then they dump it. They leave the country. This is unlike any other historical situation. You've said, "Zionism is the first liberation movement that resulted in the de-liberation of another people."

The other point that needs to be made is that we're not talking about white settlers in Africa, nor Saharan or sub-Saharan Africa. We're talking about people who are the classic victims of oppression and persecution who came to Palestine and created another victim. The uniqueness of our position is that we're the victims of the victims, which is pretty unusual, number one.

Number two, we're the first, and probably the last, liberation movement that is left to struggle in a world that is inhabited by only one superpower, that is the patron of our enemy. So we have no strategic ally, as the South Africans did, SWAPO did, the Cubans, the Nicaraguans, Guinea Bissau, they all had the presence of the Soviet Union. It's a striking fact that no successful liberation movement in the post-World War II twentieth century was successful without the Soviet Union. We are without the Soviet Union. Not that we ever had it, but it's not even present. And our environment—the South Africans had the neighboring African states—in our case, the neighboring Arab states, whether they be Syria or Jordan or Lebanon, are places where Palestinians were massacred. In the case of Syria, there's a tremendous enmity towards the national movement. That's the second unusual point.

The third unusual point is that we are a liberation movement that midway through its struggle turned itself into an independence movement, for national independence. For a long time we were conducting a struggle on two fronts in two modes. One, we were saying we were liberation. Palestine Liberation Organization, which means the liberation of Palestine. It's still called PLO. On the other hand, we were an independence movement, because we wanted national sovereignty and independence on a part of Palestine. So it's very complicated, because, finally, we are also a liberation, decolonizing movement with no sovereignty at all. All of the other movements had sovereignty. This is a unique colonialism that we've been subjected to where they have no use for us. The best Palestinian for them is either dead or gone. It's not that they want to exploit us, or that they need to keep us there in the way in Algeria or South Africa as a subclass. They do that in the West Bank and Gaza. Palestinians are building the houses for the people who are dispossessing them, the settlements. But there's no view, nor is there except amongst a few individuals, any idea of what to do with the Palestinians as human beings who are there.

The South African historian Colin Bundy is the author of a theory to deal with the problem of South Africa. He calls it "colonialism of a special type," CST in South Africa. Because you have a native white class, not settlers. But it would apply equally to Palestinians, except I think you'd have to call it "colonialism of an even more special type." It's a tremendous burden.

I sense preeminently that you're a man of letters, literature, music and that's where you're natural inclinations lie. Yet you are caught up in this political arena as the "designated Arab" for the major media. What kind of impact is that having on you?

I don't think about it very much. I don't find it either interesting or rewarding for most of the kinds of interviews and spots that you are given, the twenty-second sound bite, etc. I try not to do that any more. It doesn't strike me as…

"…What do you think of the hostages?" "What do you think of the terrorists?" are the questions posed to you.

That's right. There was a lot of interest in me during the time of the hostages, although I know next to nothing about it and it doesn't interest me. They would call and say, We would like to interview you on the *Today Show* about the release of William Mann or whoever was released before him, and I'd say, Yes, but could we also speak about the 15,000 Palestinian political prisoners who are hostages inside Israel on the West Bank and Gaza? No, no, we can't talk about that, it's a different story.

We'll need a panel.

It's the notion of designation. It's the single-minded focus on one topic which you are always required to spout. Some completely negligible stuff, just because they have to have it on the record that somebody of that kind said it. I've lost interest in that. The main thing I'm interested in now, to be perfectly honest with you, is not a political question, it's a moral question. I'm very interested and lose no opportunity to bring to the attention of intellectuals, writers, painters, artists, dramatists, etc., this issue, which affects most of them. Not just the Jews, although many of them are Jewish. But also Americans, because Americans and Jews are involved in this. The Americans are paying for the occupation of the West Bank and Gaza. And Jews, even though they're not interested and don't follow it, it is their name that is being taken, by Shamir when he says, we're doing this for the security of Israel. It's the state of the Jewish people everywhere, not just the citizens. So my sense of it is that it's therefore very important to connect Israel a) to the occupation, as South Africa was connected to apartheid, and b) to connect myself as a Palestinian and as an American with concerned Americans and Jews who are connected to it. In a certain sense, to reconnect. That's the most important thing to be done at present, I think.

There's a story that you tell that I think is revealing. You had just had a knee operation and had just gotten into a taxicab in New York and you had an exchange with the driver.

With the Israeli driver? He asked me who I was, recognized me or something. He said, I'm an Israeli. I said, fine, I'm a Palestinian. There was a pause, and then he said, I didn't serve. I refused to serve on the West Bank, and I'm here partly because of that reason. Then he said, So we're not all bad. He was very interested in testifying to me that not every Israeli could be stereotyped into the figure of the policeman with a club beating up a kid. Then he said something like, We can be friends, can't we? I said, Yes, of course. You're the type of person I would want to be friends with. It was like a strange interplanetary encounter. I got out. It was a short taxi ride. I was hobbling around with my bad leg. But it struck me that in a certain sense it was a moment lost to the future. Nothing much could come of it, a) given the situation, and b) given the fact that we're so itinerant, he was away and I was away and we just happened to encounter each other. But it left a sense of regret, that there ought to be a way of making such meetings possible in a meaningful and lasting way.

When Meir Kahane was murdered in New York, my first thoughts turned to you and the danger that you may have faced at that time. Obviously fear is related to the kind of work you're doing. How do you deal with that?

Not to think about it too much. It's probably just as dangerous for the average citizen of the Upper West Side where I live in Manhattan to cross the street as it is to be threatened by some mad zealot who wants to shoot you. I think if you dwell on any problem of that sort, then the worst is accomplished by incapacitating you. The main thing is to just keep going and to take reasonable precautions. It's harder on other people than it is on yourself. I've gotten used to it. I've been threatened by Arab groups, I'm on half a dozen death lists in the Middle East. I think the main thing is to just keep going and to remember that what you say and do means much more than whether you're safe or not.

Another hidden aspect of the question of Palestine is the Christian representation in the Palestinian movement. You yourself are a Christian, as is George Habash, Nayef Hawatmeh, and others. How would you account, and correct me if my perception is wrong, but there seems to be a disproportionate number of professors, architects, doctors, dentists, etc., from a Christian background in the foreground of the nationalist movement.

There are two classical Orientalist explanations given: Christians in the Middle East are anxious to prove themselves worthy members of the community. They fear the Sunni majority. In order to gain credentials in that community, they have to prove themselves more nationalist and more active in the national struggle than the normal Muslim would be. It's a form of overcompensation for a kind of internal anxiety that minorities always want to prove themselves. One way of doing that is to attack the majority, but in our case it is to belong to it by super-identification. The second Orientalist reason given is that the people are involved in this because Christians are higher class congenitally than Muslims. Most of them are Western educated. They speak Western languages. They come from Westernized families. Therefore, they are on a higher level than the others and feel it's important to be involved in the movement.

My sense of it is that it's a completely natural thing for a Christian and/or a Muslim to be involved in this, and if there's any particular importance to being Christian in Palestine it is obviously that many of us are quite proud of the many centuries, 2,000 years of a Christian presence in Palestine, to which we belong. This entails a special obligation to be active on the part of our national community. I think all of us feel that. I must tell you that I've been involved in this struggle for a lot of years in my life. Many members of my family have been, and I know all the people you've mentioned.

None of us has ever felt the slightest discrimination against us by the majority. I think that the last point to be made about it is the whole concept of the relationship between a minority and a majority in the Arab world is not easily perceived by a European or a Westerner, who always thinks in the categories of Western racism and Western discrimination against oppressed minorities. It doesn't work that way. I'm not saying that minorities are always wonderfully well off in the Arab world and that they haven't been oppressed; they have. But the general modus vivendum has been, in my opinion, a much more healthy and natural, easygoing one than the anxiety-laden and stressed one between minority and majority in the West.

You're fond of quoting Césaire's "There's room for everyone at the rendezvous of victory."

Yes. The whole idea of homogeneity, that if you belong to a group everybody of that group has to be exactly the same, and that only that group has the right, if it's the majority: that's completely flawed. I didn't grow up that way. I think it's important to remember that the changes in the Middle East by which states were divided from each other in the region, neighbors, Syria for the Syrians, Lebanon for the Lebanese, Jordan for the Jordanians, Egypt for the Egyptians, all of that is of quite recent vintage. When I was growing up it was possible to move from one country, Lebanon, Jordan, Syria, Palestine, Egypt, to go across them overland. It was possible to do that. All the schools I went to as a boy were full of people of different races. It was completely natural for me to be in school with Armenians, Muslims, Italians, Jews, and Greeks, because that was the Levant and that was the way we grew up. The new divisiveness and the ethnocentrism that we now find is of relatively new vintage and completely foreign to me. And I hate it. That's why Césaire's quote is so important, as a vision that there's room for all. Why does one have to be on top of the other? Why does one have to get there first and push off all the other people at the rendezvous of victory? It seems to me completely wrong to do that. One of the things I've opposed in various things I've written recently is the idea in many of the intellectual and political agendas of the oppressed that when they get to the rendezvous of victory they're going to take it out on the others. It's completely foreign to the idea of liberation. It's as if part of the privilege of winning is that you can shaft all the other people. That goes exactly against the reason for struggle itself, and is why I can't agree with it. That's another pitfall of nationalism, or what Fanon calls "pitfall of national consciousness." When national consciousness becomes an end in itself, an ethnic particularity or a racial particularity or some largely invented national essence on its own, when it becomes the program of a civilization or culture or political party, you know it's the end of human community and you get something else.

Perhaps we can close on a literary note. So much of your work is infused with poetry. You quote Neruda in an essay entitled "Yeats and Decolonization" saying "through me, freedom and the sea will call in answer to the shrouded heart."

It's a wonderful passage. I don't know how good a translation it is, or how accurate it is. The idea is that human beings are not closed receptacles, but instruments through which other things flow. The idea is of the human being as a traveler, who can have imprinted upon him or her the sights and sounds and bodies and ideas of others so that he or she could become an other and can take in as much as the sea and therefore release the shrouds and the barriers and the doors and the walls that are so much a part of human existence. That's what it's all about.

I've always thought the interesting thing about Palestine is that Palestine in a certain sense, and here's a little chauvinism, has a kind of universality to it. In fact, because of its fantastic referential power, Jerusalem as the center of the world. Jerusalem, the city from which I come, has a unique status in the world. It's not an ordinary city, at least in its existential and imaginative status. But to think that Jerusalem is just the city of one person and that it's just the place where Christianity started or only the place where the patriarchate of the Greek Orthodox Church says is the seat of its authority is a debasement of that. It has this extraordinary exfoliating power which has been betrayed by almost every political program and, in the case of Israel, sovereignty, that has taken it over. The Jordanians weren't any better. The Arab position on Jerusalem, which is to redivide it into east and west, is completely unacceptable to me. The idea is that for a place like Jerusalem you need an imaginative vision of the status of the city that can be realized in the life of the citizens of Jerusalem and not imposed on them by guards and outposts and police stations.

Armenians from historical Armenia in eastern Turkey used to make pilgrimages to Jerusalem and when they returned home, they would be called "hajji…"

The word is used in Arabic for the pilgrimage to Mecca and Medina, but also for Jerusalem. The whole idea of hijra is important in this whole concept. Emigration. Hijra and hajj, they have a relationship which is very important, to emigrate and then to return in an act of pilgrimage is very important. But one has to see both of them, return and exile, not just one.

CULTURE AND IMPERIALISM
JANUARY 18, 1993

David Barsamian: Where does *Orientalism* factor in *Culture and Imperialism*?

Edward Said: *Orientalism* did something fairly limited, although it covered a lot of ground. I was interested in Western perceptions of the Orient and in the transformation of those views into Western rule over the Orient. I limited myself to the period from about 1800 until the present, looking at the Islamic Arab world. I only looked at it from the point of view of the West, with the understanding, which has been in my opinion greatly misconstrued by critics of mine, that I was talking about an aspect of the West, not the whole West. I wasn't suggesting that the West is monolithic. But those departments of the West in England and France and America that were concerned, as a matter of policy and rule, with the Middle East.

Culture and Imperialism is in a certain sense a sequel to that in that a) I discuss other parts of the world besides the Middle East. In fact, I don't spend much time talking about the Middle East. I look at India, the subcontinent generally, a lot of Africa, the Caribbean, Australia, parts of the world where there was a major Western investment, whether through empire or direct colonialism or some combination of both, as in the case of India. That's one difference. And b) although I cover the same time period, the end of the eighteenth century to the present, the second aspect of the book which is to a certain degree dependent on *Orientalism* but goes further, is that I look at responses to the West, resistance to the West in the places I'm discussing. That is to say, unlike *Orientalism*, where I only looked at European and American writers and policies, in this case I look at the great culture of resistance that emerged in response to imperialism and grew into what in the twentieth century is called "nationalism." I look at the poets, writers, militants, and theoreticians of resistance in the Caribbean, Latin America, Africa, and Asia.

So it's not primarily through the prism of literature.

Or of the West. Although literature is given a certain privilege because my argument is that many of the attitudes, the references to the non-European world were in a certain sense fashioned and prepared by what you could call cultural documents, including literary ones, and preeminently narratives. In my view, the novel plays an extraordinarily important role in helping to create imperial attitudes towards the rest of the world. Interestingly enough, I'm not really concerned with the kind of imperialism that one finds in Russia, where the Russians simply advanced by adjacents. They moved east and south, whatever was near them. I'm much more interested in the way the Europeans, the British and the French, preeminently, were able to jump away from their shores and pursue a policy of overseas domination. So that England could hold India for 300 years at a distance of eight or nine thousand miles from its own shores.

With 100,000 people.

That's an astonishing fact. Even though there were important geographical separations between the metropolitan center and the distant colony, in some cases, for example, France and Algeria, that distant colony was absorbed and became a department of France, as Martinique and Guadeloupe are to this very day in the Caribbean. I look a great deal also at Ireland because it is the major European colony. In the book I examine the way in which Britain and France pioneered the idea of overseas settlement and domination. After 1945, with the era of decolonization, when the British and French empires were dismantled and the United States took over, you have a continuation of the same qualities.

You argue that culture made imperialism possible. You cite Blake: "the foundation of empire is art and science. Remove them or degrade them, and the empire is no more. Empire follows art and not vice versa, as Englishmen suppose."

I think one of the main flaws in the enormous literature in economics and political science and history about imperialism is that very little attention has been paid to the role of culture in keeping an empire maintained. Conrad was one of the most extraordinary witnesses to this. He understands that central to the idea of empire isn't so much profit, although profit was certainly a motive. But what distinguishes earlier empires, like the Roman or the Spanish or the Arabs, from the modern empires, of which the British and French were the great ones in the nineteenth century, is the fact that the latter ones are systematic enterprises, constantly reinvested. They're not simply arriving in a country, looting it and then leaving when the loot is exhausted. And modern empire requires, as Conrad said, an idea of service, an idea of sacrifice, an idea of redemption. Out of this you get these great, massively reinforced notions of, for example, in the case of France, the *mission civilisatrice*. That we're not there to benefit ourselves, we're there for the sake of the natives. Or, in the case of people like John Stuart Mill, that we are there because India requires us, that these are territories and peoples who beseech domination from us and that, as Kipling demonstrates in some of his work, without the English India would fall into ruin.

So it's that complex of ideas that particularly interests me. What especially was to me a great discovery was that these ideas were largely unchallenged within the metropolitan centers. Even the people today whom we admire a great deal, like De Toqueville and Mill, and the women's movement which began at the end of the nineteenth century...

And Jane Austen.

Jane Austen is a separate case. She's much earlier. But I'm talking about organized movements, the liberal movement, the progressive movement, or the working-class movement or the feminist movement. They were all imperialist by and large. There was no dissent from this. The only time that there began to be changes inside Europe and the United States was when the natives themselves in the colonies began to revolt and made it very difficult for these ideas to continue unchallenged. Then people like Sartre, in support of the Algerians, demonstrated on their behalf. But until then there was a widespread complicity, although there were some rebels, oppositional figures, like Wilfrid Scawen Blunt in England.

But behind the facade of culture, wasn't the glue that held the empire together bound by force, coercion, and intimidation?

Yes, of course. But what we need to understand is how very often the force of, say, the British army in India was very minimal in a way, considering the vast amount of territory that they administered and held. What you have instead is a program of ideological pacification whereby, for example, in India the system of education, which was promulgated in the 1830s, was really addressing the fact that the education of Indians under the British should teach the Indians the superiority of English culture over Indian culture. And of course when there was a revolt, as in the case of the famous so-called "Indian Mutiny" in 1857, then it was dealt with force, mercilessly, brutally, definitively. Then the facade could be re-erected and you could say, We're here for your sake and this is beneficial for you. So it was force, but much more important, in my opinion, than force, which was administered selectively, was the idea inculcated in the minds of the people being colonized that it was their destiny to be ruled by the West.

Don't you point out that in the case of India in the early 1800s the English novel was being studied there before it was being examined in England?

Not so much the English novel, but modern English literature was being studied in India. This was the discovery of a former student of mine, now a colleague, Gauri Viswanathan, in her book *Masks of Conquest*. What she argues is that the study of modern English literature begins in India well before it becomes a subject for university research and instruction in metropolitan England. If you didn't have culture and ideas about culture, the best that is thought and known, you'd have anarchy. You'd have, in effect, a lawless society. Those ideas came out of the Indian context, where her brother served for many years.

How do you account for the enduring interest in Joseph Conrad and his work? You often refer to _Heart of Darkness_.

It's not just _Heart of Darkness_ that I'm interested in. _Nostromo_, which I think is an equally great novel, published somewhat later, about 1904, is about Latin America. Conrad seems to me to be the most interesting witness to European imperialism. He was certainly in many ways extremely critical of the more rapacious varieties of empire. For example, of the Belgians in the Congo. But more than most people, he understood how insidiously empire infected not just the people who were subjugated by it, but the people who served it. That is to say that the idea of service had in it an illusion that, for example, in the case of the figures in _Heart of Darkness_, but also especially in _Nostromo_, could seduce and captivate one, so that in the end it was a form of universal corruption. The trouble with Conrad, in my opinion, and I point this out several times in the course of the book, is that although he was in many ways an anti-imperialist, he also thought imperialism was inevitable. He couldn't understand, as no one else in his time could either, that it was possible for natives to take over the governance of their own destiny. I'm not blaming him retrospectively. He lived in essentially a Eurocentric world. For him, although imperialism was in many cases bad, it was full of abuses, it hurt and harmed people both white and non-white, nevertheless there was no alternative to it. When it came to what is now called liberation, independence, freedom for people from colonialism and imperialism, Conrad simply couldn't get to that. That I think is his almost tragic limitation.

But ultimately his work gives assent, gives affirmation to imperialism.

Yes, and it's more complicated than that. In a certain sense what he does in his novels is to recapitulate the imperialist adventure. His novels are really about people going out, in many cases, to the hinterlands, to the "heart of darkness" in the case of Africa, to Latin America in *Nostromo*. There they imbue themselves with an idea of service, that they are there to help the people. But of course, they are in the process enriching themselves. But I wouldn't say that he endorses that. He sees it as inevitable. He doesn't criticize it as something that can be replaced by a different idea. More than most people, he had the outsider's sense that Europe was doomed in a certain sense to repeat this cycle of foreign adventure, corruption, and decline.

When you're examining these novelists, Flaubert, Balzac, Tennyson, Wordsworth, Dickens, et al., you open yourself to the criticism of putting the filters of the present on the lenses of the past.

I try not to do that. What I focus on exclusively are extremely precise indications in the texts where these writers, only a fraction of whom you've mentioned, actually say the things that I say they're saying. I'm not blaming them retrospectively. I say quite clearly in the beginning of the book that what I'm not interested in is the politics of blame. This is the way the world was. Those people and their views lost. They were defeated in the great wave of decolonization which forms the third big chapter of the book. But what I also say is I think it's wrong for us to exonerate the cultural archive of any association with this rather sordid experience of imperialism. In fact, I say that many of these writers are made more interesting by the fact that they understood and took for granted the presence of overseas colonies for the British.

For example, in *Mansfield Park* by Jane Austen, I comment on something that's in the novel. It's not something I add to it. The proprietor of the estate, which is called Mansfield Park, Sir Thomas Bertram, has to go to Antigua, where he owns a sugar plantation which is obviously run by slaves in order to replenish the coffers of Mansfield Park. So there's a certain dependency of a beautiful estate, signifying repose, calm, beauty, in England, on the sugar produce of a colony run by slaves in Antigua.

In our field, people like myself who teach literature historically allow ourselves to be curtained off from politics and history. We look at the work of art. I'm second to none in my appreciation for a work of art, and I only deal with writers whom I like, love, and admire. But I also say that in reading them it's not enough to say, "They're works of art." I try to reinsert them in their own history and to show—this is the important point—how many subsequent writers, for example, a whole slew of African writers writing after Conrad, really rewrote *Heart of Darkness*. What we're talking about is a process of writing back that took place.

So rather than say, Jane Austen's novel is really only about England, I say no, it's about the Caribbean. In order to understand it you have to understand the writing of Caribbean history by other Caribbean writers. It's not just Jane Austen's view of the Caribbean that we need. We need the other views as well. I establish what I call a reading which is based on counterpoint, many voices producing a history.

The main point is that the experience of imperialism is really an experience of interdependent histories. The history of India and the history of England have to be thought of together. I'm not a separatist. My whole effort is to integrate areas of experience that have been separated both analytically and politically, and I think that's wrong.

E. M. Forster is another writer you discuss.

In his *Howard's End* there's a reference to a plantation in Nigeria.

It's not just a reference. The Wilcoxes, the people who own Howard's End, own the Anglo-Nigerian rubber company. Their wealth is derived from Africa. But most critics of that novel, for example, Lionel Trilling's book on Forster, simply do not mention this fact. It's in the book. What I'm trying to do is to highlight these aspects of the great cultural archive of the West, as I try to look also at the cultural archive of places like Australia, North Africa, Central Africa, and elsewhere, to say, they're all there. We have to deal with this body of material. It's tremendously important. You may remember that the epigraph to *Howard's End* is "only connect." It's important to connect things with each other. That's what I'm trying to do in *Culture and Imperialism*.

So you accept the zeitgeist, you're not critical of it.

The criticism comes in the great resistance movements, which in the end defeated the empires.

The fact is that the empires didn't survive World War II. The Congress movement, which started in 1880 in India, was the very same party that took power in India after the British left in 1947. One of the points I tried to make here is that all of the great resistance movements of Africa, Asia, and Latin America traced their history back to the first people who resisted the white man coming. There's a continuity of resistance.

For example, the Algerian FLN, which defeated the French and achieved independence in 1962, saw themselves as continuing the resistance begun in 1830 by Emir Abd el-Kader in Algeria. They saw themselves as part of the same history. That's what I was trying to show. There's a continuous history of struggle. Imperialism is never the imposing of one view on another. It's a contested and joint experience. It's important to remember that.

Talking about Algeria, let's move on to Albert Camus, who you find a "very interesting figure." A Nobel Prize winner, he is celebrated as a universalist writer with some special insight into the human condition, a symbol of decency and resistance to fascism. But under your scrutiny, a very different Camus emerges.

No less a considerable writer, Camus is a wonderful stylist, certainly an exemplary novelist in many respects. He certainly talks about resistance. But what bothers me is that he is read out of his own context, his own history. Camus's history is that of a *colon*, a *pied noir*. He was born and grew up in a place very close to a city in Algeria on the coast, Annaba in Arabic, Bone by the French. It was made over into a French town in the 1880s and 1890s. His family came variously from Corsica and various parts of southern Europe and France. His novels, in my opinion, are really expressions of the colonial predicament. Meursault, in *L'Etranger* (*The Stranger*), kills the Arab, to whom Camus gives no name and no history. The whole idea at the end of the novel where Meursault is put on trial is an ideological fiction. No Frenchman was ever put on trial for killing an Arab in colonial Algeria. That's a lie. So he constructs something.

Second of all, in his later novel *La Peste* (*The Plague*), the people who die in the city are Arabs, but they're not mentioned. The only people who mattered to Camus and to the European reader of the time, and even now, are Europeans. Arabs are there to die. The story, interestingly enough, is always interpreted as a parable or an allegory of the German occupation of France. My reading of Camus, and certainly of his later stories, starts with the fact that he, in the late 1950s, was very much opposed to independence for Algeria. He in fact compared the FLN to Abdel Nasser in Egypt, after Suez, after 1956.

He said in 1957 that "as far as Algeria is concerned, national independence is an emotional formula. There has never yet been an Algerian nation."

Exactly. There had never been an Algerian nation. He denounced Muslim imperialism. So far from being an impartial observer of the human condition, Camus was a colonial witness. The irritating part of it is that he's never read that way. My kids recently in school and in college have read in their French classes *La Peste* and *L'Etranger*. In both cases, my son and my daughter were made to read Camus outside of the colonial context, with no indication of the rather contested history of which he was a part. He wasn't just a neutral observer, he was a committed anti-partisan of the FLN.

In his *Exile and Kingdom* there is a very interesting story called "The Adulterous Woman." You make a point about language.

It's not only language. This is a late story, after 1955. It's about a woman, Janine, who's married to a salesman. They go on a bus trip to the south of Algeria. She comments, as probably Camus felt at the time, that she was in a country that was hers, but there were these strange people. She doesn't know Arabic. She treats them as if they were a breed apart. They finally get to their destination, a dusty town in the south of Algeria. They spend the night. She can't sleep. She goes out at night. In a moment which has to be understood as a moment of sexual fulfillment, she lies down on the Algerian earth and engages in a ritual of communion with the land, which in a later note Camus says is a way of renewing the self, by drawing energy from the country. This is often read as a kind of existentialist parable, whereas in fact it is an assertion of a colonial right of French people, because Janine is French, to the land of Algeria, which they think is theirs to possess. I read it in that context, whereas normally it isn't read that way. I associate that with Camus's refusal to give up the idea of an Algeria that's special to France, l'Algerie française. What he's frequently quoted as having said, Michael Walzer for example quotes it all the time, is that, If in a war I have to choose between justice and correct ideas and the life of my mother if she's being threatened by terrorists, of course I'll pick my mother. But those are false choices. The choice is between the responsibility of intellectuals to justice and the truth and lying about it, which many of Camus's admirers fail to see.

Did not the French declare Arabic a foreign language in Algeria?

Arabic, by the end of World War II, had been proscribed as a language, because Algeria was considered to be a department of France.

The only place, and this has an extremely important bearing on the situation of contemporary Algeria, in which the language could be taught was in the mosque. Islam then and now is the last refuge of nationalism. The FLN takes power in 1962 and restores Arabic. There was a (I think) rather misconceived program of Arabization. Everybody had to learn Arabic. The generation of Ben Bella and Boumediene didn't know Arabic at all. Their working language was French. They could speak a patois and they could read the Koran, but they weren't able to use Arabic the way we can in the Eastern Arabic world. So they had to relearn it. In the meantime, the FLN became the party not only of the nation but also of the state. With its monopoly of power over thirty years, it became a force against which the faithful rebelled. Hence the FIS (Front Islamique du Salvation). It's a repetition of the same history.

You mentioned the responsibility of intellectuals. Who is the class that is making these representations of the literature that you contend are missing all these things, who are looking at Camus and occluding essential points. They're interpreting something that you say is there, that demonstrably is there, and they're not seeing it.

I can't really generalize in terms of class. But I can certainly say that one of the things that enables a reading of these things, that makes you pay attention to them, is the experience of decolonization. I think that if you have lived through a period of colonial struggle, you can return to these texts and read them in a way which is sensitive to precisely these points which are normally overlooked. If, on the other hand, you feel that literature is only literature and has nothing to do with anything else, then your job becomes to separate literature from the world and, in a certain sense, I believe to mutilate it and amputate from it those aspects which make it much more interesting and more worldly and more part of the struggle which was going on.

I don't advocate, and I'm very much against the teaching of literature as a form of politics. I think there's a distinction between pamphlets and novels. I don't think the classroom should become a place to advocate political ideas. I've never taught political ideas in a classroom. I believe that what I'm there to teach is the interpretation and reading of literary texts.

But it is political.

Only in one sense: it is a politics against the reading of literature which would denude it and emasculate what in the literature is profoundly contested.

But as a teacher you're making certain choices.

Of course. We all do. I wouldn't deny that. It's a choice that proposes a different reading of these classics. I don't by any means say it's the only reading. I just say it's a relevant reading, and it's the one that hasn't been addressed. I certainly don't intend to impose, because I think academic freedom is central to the issue, my reading on students and tell them if you don't read it this way you're failing the course. Quite the contrary. I want to provoke new and refreshing investigations of these texts in ways which will have them read more skeptically, more inquiringly, more searchingly. That's the point.

There have been a couple of pieces about the responsibility of intellectuals, Chomsky's being one, about speaking truth to power, and Julien Benda, in *La Trahison des Clercs* in 1928. He says, "The treason is their acceptance that intellectual activity could be harnessed to political, nationalist and racial ends." I would add to that: Why not?

They're well rewarded and celebrated by playing ball with the dominant culture.

One of the great tragedies is what happened in the Third World, the onset of nationalism. There's a difference between the nationalism of the triumphalist sort, which we see in America today as we, I don't know who this "we" is, go around proclaiming our victory in the Cold War, the right to intervene in Iraq and Panama, and that of which Fanon spoke in *The Wretched of the Earth*, which was the nationalism which resists colonization and imperialism. But what interests me a great deal is that when nationalism is triumphant, and independence is achieved, too often nationalism can sink back down into a kind of tribalism, atavism, statism, and along with that becomes, for example in many parts of the Arab world today, a neo-imperialist state, still controlled by outside powers and in which the ruling elite are in effect agents and clients of one of the dominant powers. This I think was quite carefully prophesied by many of the early nationalist writers in the Third World. This is often forgotten. It's always argued by people like Elie Kedourie and others in the West that nationalism is a Western invention. What you have in places like Algeria and India are imitations of the West. But what is the interesting thing is that if you look carefully at the history of this kind of resisting nationalism that I discuss in the book, you find that many of its earliest adherents warned against the abuses of nationalism. For example, Fanon says, We aren't going to fight this revolution against the French in order to replace the French policeman with an Algerian policeman. That's not the point. We are looking for liberation. Liberation is much more than becoming a mirror image of the white man whom we've thrown out and just replacing him and using his authority. So I'm very interested in that distinction, between liberation and a kind of mindless nationalism.

You also point out that the imperial theory that underlies colonial conquest continues today. How does it manifest itself, in culture particularly?

In the book I talk mainly about the public sphere in America. First of all there was a fairly pronounced sense of international mission after World War II where the United States thought of itself as being the inheritor of the British and French, the great Western empires. That was certainly the case in Latin America, in Southeast Asia, where the United States in effect followed other colonial powers. In the case of Vietnam it followed the French and went through the same disastrous course. One cycle of imperialist history follows another.

Number two, it began to circulate also in the media and in the academy that there was a whole theory of American developmental science, the developmental theorists of the 1950s and 1960s, the idea that we have to go into the world and develop the non-developed. We have to provide them with models for economic takeoff, the Walt Rostow notion. It was very brilliantly parodied in the case of Graham Greene's novel *The Quiet American*, which is really a satire on the Cold War, the American in Vietnam, Pyle, who really is providing the third way.

Neither the old colonial way nor the communist way, the ideology of the Cold War is very important here, but there's a new way, which is ours. That produces many of the policies and revolts, one thinks of Indonesia, the Philippines, the Middle East and various parts of it in 1958, the earliest American postwar interventions, which really begin in Greece and Turkey right after World War II, and the idea that America is the world's policeman.

Third, you find it in the public rhetoric of the State Department and the intellectual elite in this country. We have a mission to the world. It's echoed and re-echoed by the media. The assumptions of the media are that we are the impartial observers of the world and that there's a sense in which being a newspaper person is being a witness of power and an emissary of the United States in these places, like Baghdad, etc.

The result is a very powerful ideological system, which Chomsky has talked about brilliantly, which I think is central to the education of every American. It's based upon a great deal of ignorance about the rest of the world and very little geographical knowledge of what the rest of the world is all about. My work is very concerned with geographical knowledge. One of the interesting distinctions between America and the classical empires of the nineteenth century in Britain and France is that there was first of all contiguity. There was a sense in which France was close to North Africa. There was a connection between England and the empire of the East through Suez, the Gulf, etc. There was a colonial establishment. America has none of that. There is, on the contrary, abstract expertise, people who learn social science techniques, who can manipulate numbers, use computers, etc., but have a tremendous geographical ignorance. The United States is extremely insulated, a very provincial country in many ways. It produces these experts who are retooled for service first in Vietnam, in Latin America, in the Middle East. The result is a policy of violence on the one hand and a kind of incoherent lurching around with tremendously damaging results. It's forgotten by most Americans, many of my students don't even know about Vietnam, that the United States cost a million Vietnamese lives. That's forgotten. Jimmy Carter said it was a case of "mutual destruction." There's no comparison between the destruction of Vietnam and the losses sustained by the United States as an invading imperial force.

Last, and most important, there's been a banishment, a kind of intellectual exclusion of the notion of imperialism. The imperialists are the British and the French. We're something different. We don't have an empire. We don't have an India. But the reality is, through the transnational corporations, through the media, through the military, the United States has what Richard Barnet calls "global reach." It's the last remaining global power.

People like V. S. Naipaul say, "That's all over."

Imperialism is finished. We're now in a new era, and look at the mess. In his work that's often quoted, *Among the Believers*, here is Naipaul the novelist posing as Islamicist, sociologist, and psychologist. He travels to Iran, Pakistan, Indonesia, and Malaysia. He describes Muslims: "Their rage, the rage of a pastoral people with limited skills, limited money and a limited grasp of the world, is comprehensive. Now they have a weapon, Islam. It is their way of getting even with the world. It serves their grief, their feeling of inadequacy, their social rage, and racial hate."

Naipaul is an interesting figure. First of all, he's a very gifted writer. There's no question about it. He's also, being a man of color, a wonderful case in point, as Irving Howe did when he reviewed the novel *A Bend in the River* when it came out in 1979 in the *New York Times*, he said, This is a man who's from the Third World. He's Indian, from the subcontinent, but his family lived in Trinidad and he grew up there. He's cited along with people like Fuad Ajami as witnesses. They know what they're talking about. And they say that the place is a filthy mess. Naipaul encourages that.

I have no problem with Naipaul saying the things that he wants to say. Everybody's entitled to say what he sees. And of course the evidence of his senses is such as it is. We know, however, that he's a very lazy traveler, whose information about the countries he visits is extremely incomplete. He should write and publish, and I think people should read him and criticize him. But one should have some awareness of two things that he does that are particularly pernicious. Number one, he doesn't give a full picture of the history that produced in many cases the real mess that is to be found in countries like Iran. Iran is not just a place where there's a gratuitous emergence of Islam. It comes after a particular history with the West, a prolonged, losing encounter. The opium wars, the oil concessions, the reign of the Shah. What we have now in Iran is a response to it. So he misses that entirely. He leaves those things out. He makes it seem as if these are essentially Muslim characteristics.

And number two, much more important, is that Naipaul never gives us any indication that there's anything else in these countries except that. Islam is now the bogeyman of the West. This last summer there was a headline in the *Washington Post* that said that Islam replaces communism as the enemy of the West. This idea of some monolithic, finally undistinguished and indistinguishable form called Islam becomes a repository for all evil in the world. Without an awareness—and this is the point—of not only the monolithic quality but that within Islam and the Islamic world there are many currents, many oppositions. There are secular people who are trying to fight the brotherhoods, the jihads, Hezbollah, Hamas. These are quite different from each other. Hamas is very different from Hezbollah. The movement in Sudan run by Hassan al-Turabi is very different from the Muslim Brotherhood in Egypt, and so on.

There's very little attention paid to the other forms of fundamentalism that exist. For example, there is Jewish fundamentalism. Israel is a fundamentalist country, in many ways as terrifying to me, as a non-Jew, as Iran is. That invidiously is never discussed. Israel is ruled according to theocratic laws that forbid certain things on the Sabbath, that censor music because it's considered to be too Christian, in some instances, that proscribe composers like Wagner, that lay down very strict laws about who is a Jew and who isn't a Jew, etc. That's completely excluded from mainstream discussion. I am a secular person. I'm against any kind of religious politics. But I'm not alone. And if one is going to talk about Islam the way Naipaul does, he ought to talk about it in a much fuller and truer context than the one he engineers. For in the end it is a kind of opportunism, because it will sell and it's easy to do.

To what do you ascribe the appeal of Islam in such countries today as Algeria, Jordan, Tunisia, and especially in Egypt, where there are some very serious problems?

I think first of all it's a failure of the secular modernizing movements that came to power after World War II in reaction to imperialism. These brought very few solutions. They were unable to face the demographic explosion. They were unable to face the democratization and empowerment of the population that occurred after liberation. For example, in Egypt, for the first time in Egyptian history, every Egyptian was entitled to a full education. What is often forgotten is that the Islamic revival comes on the heels and as a result of a tremendously successful campaign against illiteracy. These are movements not run by illiterates. They're run by doctors and lawyers. These Islamic movements, which are very different in each place, are very often contested by a quite vibrant secular culture.

Crucially, the movements are occurring in countries, like Egypt, Algeria, Jordan, and Saudi Arabia, whose rulers are considered to be allies of the West. Take the alienation felt by people in Egypt who saw Sadat coddled by the United States, making peace with Israel, selling his integrity, admittedly with a great deal of panache and a great mastery of public relations, but nonetheless giving up Egyptian priorities to those priorities set by the United States. This induces a sense not only of hopelessness and desperation, but a sense of anger which is fueled by these Islamic movements.

Last and most important, the Islamic revival in the Arab world largely occurs in countries where democracy had been abrogated by virtue of the priorities of the national security state. Here Israel plays a very important role. This is often forgotten. The presence of Israel, a theocratic, military state, a Sparta, that is imposed upon the region—I'm not talking just about the Palestinians, whose society it destroys, its country, its land, it's been in occupation for over twenty-five years—but also its invasions, its incursions in Lebanon, in Jordan, in Syria, in Tunisia. It has overflown Saudi Arabia many times. It has attacked Iraq. Israel is a regional superpower. This sense of Israel and the United States as victimizing at will the Arab heartland has forced people to go back to nourishing roots in the native culture, which is Islamic.

Kind of an autochthonous, indigenous response.

It's a response to that. It's deeply flawed, in my opinion. In many cases it's reactionary. But it has objective causes. It's not some evil essentialism, as it's often portrayed in the press here. You read Bernard Lewis and he talks about the "Roots of Muslim Rage" in the *Atlantic Monthly*, and you get the sense that Muslims are just mad at modernity, as if modernity were some vague force that they want to attack and revile in order to go back to the seventh century. That is part of the picture. The descriptions of Islam in the West are part of the very same problem that Muslims throughout the Arabic world and the Islamic world generally, whether in Pakistan, Bangladesh, or Iran, are fighting. There's been very little attention paid to an understanding of Islam and a sense of wanting to have a dialogue with it. On the contrary, there are vast legions of reporters, and here's where in my opinion the laziness and mediocrity of the Western media is very much to blame, as well as the so-called intellectual experts who lend themselves to this sort of thing. Their main job, whether through the normal television documentaries and news programs that we see, is to foreshorten, compress, reduce, caricature even, in order to produce a sound bite. You can even see this in films. I remember the week before Christmas I saw at least three movies, *Delta Force* was one, on television which were all about killing "terrorists" who were Muslim and Arab at the same time. The idea of killing Arabs and Muslims is legitimized by the popular culture. This is part of the atmosphere which we need to look at.

I'm very interested that you mentioned the popular culture. You are perceived as someone who is immersed in the highbrow culture. You're an academic. But yes, there is *Delta Force*. Then, there is *Iron Eagle*, which

is one of the most extraordinary of this genre. I was asked to give a talk on representations of Arabs and Islam in the media at the University of Colorado at Boulder during what is curiously called "Arab Awareness Week." So I checked out a lot of videos and went through them. In *Iron Eagle*, an American teenager steals an F-16 in Arizona and somehow flies nonstop to the Middle East, a remarkable achievement. He kills an entire army of fanatical Arabs, who are holding his father hostage. He rescues his father and brings him back to Arizona.

My favorite is *Black Sunday*. Arabs will stoop to nothing. This is the ultimate in sinister activity: they want to disrupt and bomb the Super Bowl, the Vatican of American culture.

There's a whole range of these films. The terrorists, incidentally, are enormously incompetent. They can't shoot straight. They can't operate equipment. There's one American or one Israeli holding off a hundred Arab terrorists.

By the way, I don't know whether you're aware of this, but most of the terrorists, the Muslims and the Arabs, are played by Israelis. It's quite astonishing. They never use Arab actors. I don't think they could find any Arab actors to play these parts. There's a small but thriving industry in Israel of producing extras and stand-ins for these roles who play the Arabs who are being shot and killed. Two or three Americans versus hundreds, maybe thousands of Arabs who can't do anything right.

In addition to being portrayed as totally incompetent, Arabs never have a normal conversation. They scream at one another. They bark and shout.

It's all probably put down in the popular mind, such as it is, to Koranic imprecations, Koranic curses. That's all they ever speak. The word "Koranic" is wonderful, because it includes almost everything you don't like.

There have been some middlebrow films as well, *Lawrence of Arabia* and *The Sheltering Sky*. The pattern continues. *Patriot Games* is a recent film with Harrison Ford in which IRA terrorists are trained by Libyans in the desert. You've commented that there are only a few Arabic words that have entered the English language in the twentieth century, such as *jihad*, *intifada*, *harem*, and *sheikh*. I think that really shows the contrast: one is violence and the other is sensuality.

Intifada is a recent word associated with a particular political uprising, which I think on the whole is positive, a revolt against colonial occupation. It was taken up all through some of the great uprisings in the Third World and the Second World, Eastern Europe and the non-European world generally during the late 1980s. People in Prague were wearing intifada T-shirts in the Velvet Revolution. When I was in South Africa last year, one of the striking things was that, largely because Mandela made the connection, there was a very warm sense of association between Palestinians fighting against Israeli occupation and the struggle against apartheid in South Africa. The intifada was really the crucial point.

In the process of preparing for that talk that I mentioned, I went to the public library to do some research. Boulder is a fairly progressive, liberal town. I examined what they had in the public library. I discovered they had 257 books on Christianity, 160 on Judaism, 63 on Islam. Given the fact that there are very few Muslims in Boulder, I'd say that's a

pretty generous selection of books on Islam. But then you look at some of the titles and come to some other conclusions. Some of them are: *The Islamic Bomb, March of Islam, Militant Islam, Holy Terror: Inside the World of Islamic Terror, Sacred Rage, The Crusade of Modern Islam, Among the Believers,* the Naipaul book, and my particular favorite, *Banditry in Islam.* I then looked at the Christian and Judaic titles, expecting to find *The Judaic Bomb, Banditry in Christendom.* Not one.

I think we have a sense here that I've been very critical of, both this phenomenon that you're talking about, but also on the other side. The Arab and Islamic world has not really paid enough attention to this. There needs to be an effort made by Arab intellectuals or Islamic intellectuals to address the West. The books you referred to should be refuted, of course. But also there should be an attempt to put forward an alternative view of Islam which not only refutes these but embodies the reality of Islam, which is very various and on the whole quite benign. I was interested during the 1492–1992 commemorations of the past year that there was very little effort made by the Arab countries in the West to describe Andalusian civilization, which is one of the high points in the human adventure because of its ecumenism, the splendor of its aesthetic and intellectual achievements, but also that it provided a kind of counter model to the Islam that is argued today as being the essential one. Namely, an Islam that is not only tolerant but actually encouraged coexistence of the various communities. This is the model.

Against it, I think largely because of the struggle between the Palestinians and Israel, a new view of Islam has emerged as essentially intolerant, reactionary, and above all a chauvinist religion which cannot tolerate the outsider. But there's a difference between an outsider in the general sense, which is the way Bernard Lewis always speaks about it, and the outsider as represented by Israel. Israel is after all an incursion against not an Arab territory but a territory that was ecumenical.

When I grew up in Palestine it was a place in which the three faiths lived, perhaps not perfectly, but certainly better than they lived in Europe at the same time. I was born at the end of 1935. During that time, as the Jews were about to be slaughtered in Europe, there were small Jewish communities in Palestine. At the time one didn't know that they were planning to become much larger communities, and in fact take over the country from the original inhabitants, the Palestinians. But instead you get an image of Islam that is bent upon the destruction of the Other. This continued portrait of Islam has never really, in my opinion, been responded to by Muslims themselves in the West, who think it's all just propaganda. I'm very critical of the Arab states, for example, in their information policy, not showing that this is not only wrong but that in fact one can argue with it. I'm an optimist. I think people can be made to change their minds and that experiencing a different and alternative view of the Islamic and Arab world can in fact open people's minds in the West to another perspective.

You have observed that in many Arab colleges and universities there are no departments that study the United States?

There isn't a single one in any Arab university today that is exclusively devoted to the study of the West, or in particular the United States. I mentioned this in Birzeit University (West Bank) on my trip in June of 1992. I was told, not only do we not have a department of American Studies here, given that the United States is the most powerful outside force in the region, we don't even have a department of

Hebrew and Israeli Studies. After all, Israel is the occupying power. Some attention should be paid to the systematic study of the state and its society as it impinges on Arab life. That hasn't occurred yet. These are all parts of the legacy of imperialism.

There's a certain chauvinism there, too.

It's not only chauvinism, but there's a certain sense that you shouldn't defy it. The absence of defiance bothers me a great deal. What distinguishes people in the contemporary Arab world from the period of the 1950s and 1960s and certainly the 1930s and 1940s is an attitude of wanting to challenge imperialism. Now there's a great fear. The Palestinians and others run to the United States as if it were the court of last resort and the true friend of justice. There is very little awareness. Certainly this is the case in the negotiations in Washington and Madrid. There's very little sense of the history of the United States. There was Baker, who said, Oh, yes, we really want you in the peace talks, that really was a word that could be taken at face value, and it proved a tremendous disappointment.

This may be a generalization. I haven't traveled extensively in the Arab world, but in the contact that I have had there's a sense that the Arabs, particularly the Palestinians, are the aggrieved party, they have been trodden upon savagely. You could make a strong case for that. And that right is on their side and it will be discovered. They don't have to make a strong case.

That's absolutely right. There's a sense in which the sense of being right and the rightness of the case requires no further action.

Allah Kareem is sort of the abiding philosophy.

A very un-Gramscian attitude, I'm afraid.

Let's move to your December 1992 *Harper's* article, "Palestine, Then and Now." It was very moving. I was very touched by it. There was a strong sense of sadness and sorrow permeating the piece. You used such adjectives as "mournful," "gloomy," and "melancholy." "Acre is a very sad place." It was a kind of "bury the dead" journey. It was like a testimony. You were linking your children with your past.

I thought it was important for them to see it.

They've never been to Palestine. They've never seen where I was born and grew up. I'm not a great believer in roots, to be honest. I think roots can be overstated. But Palestine is an unusual place. Whether you are from there or not, it's certainly something that affects you. There's been a tremendous amount of attention, alas, a lot of it due to Israeli propaganda, to the situation in the Middle East. So my kids grew up knowing about Palestine essentially through these secondhand reflections of it that you see in the media, reading about it, and having been, as they had been, to countries like Egypt and Lebanon and Jordan. They had a sense of belonging to a community but no sense of the particularity of a community to which their father belonged. So in that sense it was very important.

I found writing about the experience very difficult. I think I got about 10 or 15 percent of the barrage of impressions I received and memories that were stimulated by that trip. We were there for about ten days, and we went everywhere. So it was difficult to choose. There were two contradictory feelings that I had overall. One was a sense of pleasure at coming back to a place which in a certain sense I could still recognize. I was aware of the extent to which Palestine had been transformed into Israel. I'm not from the West Bank, but from what became in 1948 Israel, West Jerusalem, Talbiya. My mother's from Nazareth, which is also part of Israel. I remember Haifa, Jaffa, that's the geography of my childhood. To see that it survived and that there was a recognizable Arab presence there, despite the enormous upheavals and transformations of the last forty years was heartening.

On the other hand, it was very difficult for me to note the way in which the place had become another country, in some instances a kind of ersatz European country. Talbiya looks like an elegant Zurich suburb. There were no Arabs there. We went to Safad, which is where my uncle used to live, a place we used to visit, the last time I was there in 1946. I visited in 1992, forty-six years later, there wasn't a single Arab in sight. They had all been driven out. So these are sites of catastrophe for me. Of course, in the general political economy of memory and recollection that exists in public culture in the West, there's no room for the Palestinian experience of loss. So it was very hard.

Interestingly, I might add that the article you saw in *Harper's* brought forth a number of responses from friends who wrote telling me how much they enjoyed reading about it and how they were stirred and saddened by it. But the thing I was unprepared for was that it seemed to infuriate a lot of pro-Israelis, who wrote the most angry, appalling letters. After all, I was only describing a trip. They were angry that I should even say anything like this. One person who claimed to be a psychiatrist, for example, prescribed a psychiatric hospital for me, that I should be locked up. Others accused me of lying. The most extraordinary propaganda, hysterical, rabid letters to *Harper's* and to me. It shows the extent to which in the official Zionist discourse the presence of a Palestinian voice or a Palestinian narrative is simply unacceptable. I think it should be noted that there still isn't allowed a presence, even though this discourse is responsible for the destruction of Palestine and the horrors meted out onto a population of almost five million people today. There's no responsibility taken for it. I find that very disheartening.

I think you might also be underestimating your own position. I remember when you came to Boulder in 1990 and you were astonished that your talk was being picketed and people were handing out leaflets denouncing you. You are a significant figure, and you will attract this kind of attention.

But even so, it strikes me as inhumane and intolerant. If Muslims did this, as they have done, for example, to Salman Rushdie, there's a chorus of protest saying, you cannot prevent somebody from speaking. But this continues against Palestinians. There are constant attempts to silence, to vilify, to blackmail, to make life miserable for anybody who dares speak out. I find that absolutely appalling. Especially since a lot of the time it's accompanied by moralistic piety about the necessity to remember the horrors of the past and the Jewish experience, with which I completely agree. But if you dare say something about an attendant holocaust, perhaps not a holocaust but a catastrophe, we call it the *nakba*, catastrophe, that occurred for us as a result of the Holocaust, the destruction of Palestine, that's not permitted. And the violence and the anger and the poison that's spewed out is terrifying.

Let's go back to your visit to Israel and Palestine. You arrive at Lad airport, outside Tel Aviv. There's a tremendous sense of apprehension and

anxiety. You're met by Mohammed Miari, who is an Arab-Israeli member of the Knesset.

This was about ten days before the elections. Unfortunately, Miari was not reelected.

But you observed the ease with which he spoke Hebrew and moved about among the Israelis and you said, "I was learning the reality of things." But you really didn't pursue that. Why not?

It was difficult to describe it. I thought that Palestinians lived, as indeed they do, as a subservient minority population in their own country. That's certainly true. Arab villages inside Israel are poorer. Education is given a lot less money than education for the Jewish citizens of Israel. Yet, what I was unprepared for was the general sense, I wouldn't call it defiance, in which Palestinians who are Israeli citizens live in the state in a contestatory way. But they are by no means submissive and meek. There's a certain amount of resistance that they put up. Miari is a perfect example. He's a fighter in the Knesset. He belongs to a tiny minority of five or six Palestinian members in an overwhelmingly Jewish parliamentary house, the Knesset. But he's far from silent. Never having seen Palestinians with Israelis inside Israel, I was surprised and heartened. It's a mundane observation, but I thought it was quite remarkable. And I thought that Palestinians would try to be unobtrusive. I never felt that. I felt that Palestinians inside Israel acted and spoke as if it was their country. They weren't there on tolerance or on sufferance. They were there because they belonged there. I was glad to see that. I certainly felt that they should feel and act that way, and they did. I had no idea what it was like.

The visit to your family home in Jerusalem is described in very poignant terms. It's an irony that Swift would have appreciated, for the house you were born in today houses the International Christian Embassy, a fundamentalist Christian group which is pro-Zionist. You said, "anger and melancholy overtook me, so that when an American woman came out of the house with an armful of laundry and asked if she could help, I could not bring myself to ask to go inside."

That was the one place where I felt that I didn't penetrate enough into my own past. I felt that throughout Palestine and Israel, when we were wandering around to sites that were important to me whether for memory or places like Hebron because of political and more recent associations, I ventured into these places for the first time with a great deal of interest and desire to know. Here I felt something I didn't feel anywhere else in Palestine. I didn't want to know. I simply did not want to go inside the house, although my kids urged me to go in. I pointed out the window of the room in which I was born, which you could see from the outside of the house, and said to them that that was where I was born. They said, "Daddy, don't you want to go in and look at it?" I said, No, I didn't. It was as if there was a part of my past which was really over and associated with the fall of Palestine which I couldn't reinvestigate, I couldn't visit once again. It was enough to see it from the outside, somehow. That sort of made the point for me.

One of the subheadings in the essay is "Descending into Gaza." I don't think the metaphor was lost on you. It is a descent.

It's the most terrifying place I've ever been in.

Before we went—I didn't say this in the article—the young Palestinian who drove us to Gaza from Jerusalem said to my wife and daughter, "You can't go to Gaza looking the way you do, wearing Western dress. You really have to be veiled. You have to cover your head and arms." It was midsummer, a hot day. I said, "We weren't told this before." He said, "Well, they didn't tell you. Gaza is a very violent place, and anybody who strays from the straight and narrow equally Arab or Israeli gets stoned. You shouldn't wear dark glasses in Gaza, because then they'll immediately know you're a foreigner and maybe an Israeli spy and they'll gang up on you." So there's this whole mythology about Gaza which predisposes you to dislike it. In effect, when you go in there it's a horrifyingly sad place because of the desperation and misery of the way people live. I was unprepared for camps that are much worse than anything I saw in South Africa. I felt that the imposed regime of inhumanity and primitive, even barbarian absence of amenities are a great crime against humanity, imposed ultimately by the Israelis. There's nobody else who rules there. So that the intransigence and rebelliousness of many of the people, certainly the young men we saw, is exactly explainable by those circumstances. Against which no one speaks out except a few people like Gloria Emerson. Nobody talks about Gaza.

You wrote, "Nothing I saw in South Africa can compare with Gaza in misery. Yet Israel has been spared universal criticism as South Africa has not. Somehow Israel is viewed as unconnected to U.S. practices." "Somehow" is a bit imprecise. It's not magic.

No, it isn't. I can't understand it, that's why I used "somehow." It is something I can't explain. People who know what Gaza is like find it very difficult to connect the situation in Gaza with the practices of the Israeli government. I'm surprised that there hasn't been, just as I

was surprised that there hadn't been a major Western campaign by
academics against the closure of the educational institutions of the
West Bank and Gaza, that more people haven't tried to draw attention to this fact. Even in the recent business of the deportations,
most of them are from Gaza. Nobody in any of the media reports
that I saw, associated the type of resistance practiced by the people of
Gaza with the situation there which has been created by the Israelis,
who have tried to reduce Gazans to an animal-like existence. Nobody made that point. I find that extraordinary.

**As Prime Minister Rabin said, the world is hypocritical when it comes to
the deportations. There's all this hollering and screaming about 415
Palestinian deportees. Where was the world when 300,000 Palestinians
were deported from Kuwait? You have to agree with him.**

Yes, he's exactly right. The difference is, of course, that first of all Israel is responsible for the destruction of an entire country, which occurred in 1948, and the expulsion of most of its population, and
second, Israel has been in colonial occupation flaunting dozens of UN
Security Council resolutions on the West Bank and Gaza since 1967.
Number three, a much more important point for me, the Kuwaitis
and their response to the Palestinians are disgraceful. The Kuwaitis do
not have a high standing in the West. They're a figure of fun. They are
a corrupt and mediocre lot. I'm talking about the ruling families who
run the country. And they deserve everything they get. They had a war
fought on their behalf by the United States, of course because of their
oil. That's about it, and nobody's giving them more credit.

Israel is the moral godchild of the West. Israel is celebrated,
saluted, given hundreds of millions of dollars. $77 billion have been

vouchsafed to Israeli citizens since 1967 by the United States alone. And therefore is answerable to criticism of this sort. It is in defiance of United Nations resolutions. So I think that Rabin is only partly right. He, in my opinion, is a war criminal in any case, because he was personally responsible for turning 50,000 Palestinians of Lydda and Ramla into refugees in 1948. He talked about it in his memoirs. Nobody ever asked him that question. "Don't you see, Mr. Rabin, a continuity between what you did in 1948 in the army, in the Haganah, and what you've done now?" There is a continuity. This is the same man who expelled 50,000 people in 1948 and has recently kicked out 415. What's even more disgraceful is that Rabin is considered to be a man of the left. He's a member of the Socialist International. In his cabinet, many leftwingers, the Meretz party, voted along with him for the deportations. In the process nobody has inquired as to why there is this extraordinary congruence between liberal and left on the one hand and deportation and expulsion on the other.

I think here it's important to note that the idea of getting rid of the Palestinians has been a constant in Zionist thought since the early twentieth century, whether of the left, the right, or the center. Every major Zionist thinker has always talked about the transfer of the Palestinians, the expulsion of the Palestinians, getting rid of them, spiriting them away. So it's a continuity which was there from the very beginning. It's not some aberration on the part of Rabin.

You've said that the enemy of the Palestinians, in the end, is not to be forgotten or marginalized, but that "it is silence: to be aware and to turn away." I would add that time is also your enemy.

I know. Time is our enemy. But on the other hand, one of the major achievements of Palestinian struggle in the last twenty years has been that more and more Palestinians are dedicated to remaining on the land. As long as we're there, we provide a problem for them. That's the main thing. There's no doubt in my mind that ultimately they want to get rid of us. The idea that there's some notion that Shamir wanted to forever hold on to the land of Israel while Rabin is different—that's tommyrot. He talks a different line. He's much more plausible when it comes to *hasbara*; information in the West for the goyim, but basically it's the same idea. The best thing that will happen to the Palestinians is to get rid of them. If they won't be gotten rid of, we'll sign an agreement with them that will make their lives so intolerable that in the end they will die to get out. That is in my opinion the plan. Anything that you hear about reconciliation and peace is the talk only of a marginal few. In the mainstream is basically a notion of fundamental apartheid, that the Palestinians have got to go.

Why do I say this? Not because I'm angry at them or because I've lost hope, but largely because there is no appreciable segment of Israeli public opinion that has ever voiced anything but these views of Palestinians. There are a few visionaries, people like Professor Shahak, Professor Liebovitz, the members of B'Tselem, the human rights observer group, etc. They believe in coexistence with the Palestinians on the basis of equality. But the basic Zionist premise, which runs not only the negotiations but the status quo in terms of the current situation, is that Palestinians have to be inferior and if possible out of there. There has never been a credible alternative within the mainstream of Zionist thinking. That's as true of American Jews who are Zionists as it is of Israeli Jews.

It's the process exemplified in that term you often heard in Gaza, "*maut batiq*," slow death.

Exactly.

Stephen Daedalus in *Ulysses* talks about history as "a nightmare from which I am trying to awake." When you're awake what do you see?

I don't think history's a nightmare, unlike Stephen Daedalus. I don't take that view. I think history is a place of many possibilities. I don't think in the present political setup either in the Middle East or in the United States that any real change is going to happen. It can only happen very slowly and as a result of education. Education is a central instrument in all of this. Without a self-conscious, skeptical, democratically-minded citizenry, there's no hope for any political change for the better, in this country or in the Middle East. That is occurring only very slowly.

You conclude the *Harper's* piece with, "I would find it very hard to live there. I think exile seems to be a more liberated state. But I can feel and sometimes see a different future as I couldn't before." That reminded me of a T. S. Eliot line you've quoted elsewhere: "Here the impossible union of separate spheres of existence is actual. Here the past and future are conquered and reconciled." That's the kind of vision you have.

Absolutely. And I think it's possible through vision. That's why I think culture is so important. It provides a visionary alternative, a distinction between the this-worldness and the blockage that one sees so much in the world of the everyday, in which we live, which doesn't allow us to see beyond the impossible odds in power and status that are stacked, for example, against Palestinians, and the possibility of dreaming a different dream and seeing an alternative to all this. I learned this many years ago from a great English critic, Raymond Williams, who more than anyone else taught me the notion of always thinking the alternative. Not so much only the dream, which is rather other-worldly, but to every situation, no matter how much dominated it is, there's always an alternative. What one must train oneself is to think the alternative, and not to think the accepted and the status quo or to believe that the present is frozen.

THE ISRAEL/PLO ACCORD:
A CRITICAL ASSESSMENT

SEPTEMBER 27, 1993

David Barsamian: The accord that was signed in Washington on September 13 between the Israeli government and the PLO has been hailed by *Time* magazine, for example, as "a historic breakthrough." Thomas Friedman in the *New York Times* called it "the Middle East equivalent of the fall of the Berlin Wall." The deal, he said, represents "the triumph of realism over fanaticism and political courage over political cowardice." What is your reading of what happened in Washington?

Edward Said: I think it is a historic breakthrough of enormous proportions, but principally for the Palestinians, it's an instrument of capitulation. Actually, Thomas Friedman, who has been celebrating the accord, every so often lets by a more honest appraisal of it. In one of his articles he calls it the Palestinian "surrender." I think that's very true. There are certain positive things about it which I'll come to in a moment, but I think it's important to quote other sources than the chorus of mindless approval. For example, on a television program three weeks ago, ex-Secretary of State James Baker was being needled by Cokie Roberts, who kept saying, Why should Israel trust the PLO? After all, Arafat is a terrorist. They never keep their promises. And so on. Rather exasperated, he said, Cokie, there's no reason why they should trust or not trust Arafat. The fact is, they haven't given anything up. And in a BBC interview which I did at the same time, back to back, with Amos Oz, who is a "dovish" Israeli, he was asked by the BBC's Michael Ignatieff, What do you think about this accord? This was kind of a summary statement. Oz said, "Well, September 13, 1993, is the day of the second greatest victory of Zionism, the first one being the establishment of the state in 1948." I think to a certain degree there's something to all of these comments.

As for the positive elements of the accord, of course there is the recognition of the PLO by Israel. But the PLO is recognized as "the" representative, and not the single, the sole legitimate representative of the Palestinian people. But if you look at it just that way, then you're really missing the wrapping in which this recognition comes, because on the other side, the Palestinian recognition of Israel and its right to exist, a formula which doesn't exist in international relations, by the way, also is accompanied by a whole series of renunciations by the PLO, which includes renunciation of violence and terrorism, suggesting, of course, that the PLO was a terrorist organization and had now reformed itself, whereas to its people and to most of the world, excluding the U.S. and Israel, the PLO is a national liberation organization and a national authority. So the characterization of all acts of violence, which some might interpret as resistance against much greater Israeli violence, has been renounced and admitted to as terrorism and violence. In my opinion it's a shameful characterization of the history of the Palestinian resistance movement, which for at least a hundred years now has been unsuccessfully resisting the Zionist invasion of Palestine and has never been able, alas, to take back any territory.

In addition, in the recognition there is the notion that the PLO and Israel will now negotiate on the basis of Resolutions 242 and 338, resolutions which in fact do not mention Palestinians at all. And in the process of doing this, as subsequent history has proved, the PLO is giving up all the other resolutions passed by the UN since 1948, including and above all, Resolution 194, which says that Palestinian refugees made refugees by Israel in 1948 are entitled to compensation or repatriation. Even the U.S. has voted for this. Every year it's been passed by the General Assembly. What we now learn is that both the Israeli and the PLO representatives at the UN are now meeting to modify, repeal, renegotiate all of these UN resolutions, which include those condemning Israel for the settlements, for the annexation of Jerusalem and the Golan Heights, the mistreatment of its civilian population under occupation, and so on, which are now slowly being given up by the PLO.

In addition, and this is something deeply troubling to me, the PLO has accepted the notion that it's not negotiating for the national rights of the Palestinians and self-determination. What it's negotiating for is the interim limited self-rule of the residents of the West Bank and Gaza. So both in the exchange of letters and in the declaration of principles which Israel and the PLO signed on that day, there's no mention of the Palestinians who do not reside on the West Bank and Gaza. This is over 50 percent of the Palestinian population, which are now stateless people in Lebanon, Syria, 1.4 million in Jordan, and so on. And all of that's been thrown away.

The actual ceremony itself, if one watched it, and I did—I had been invited but refused to attend because for me it wasn't an occasion of celebration but an occasion for mourning—was, I thought, quite tawdry. In the first place, there was Clinton, like a Roman emperor bringing two vassal kings to his imperial court and making them shake hands in front of him. Then there was the fashion show parade of star personalities brought in. Then, and most distressing of all, were the speeches, in which Israeli prime minister Rabin gave [what should have been] the Palestinian speech, full of anguish, Hamlet's anxiety and uncertainty, the loss, the sacrifice, and so on. In the end I felt sorry for Israel. Arafat's speech was in fact written by businessmen and was a businessman's speech, with all the flair of a rental agreement. It was really quite awful. And he didn't even mention anything about the sacrifices of the Palestinian people; he didn't even mention the Palestinian people in any serious way. I thought therefore that the occasion was an extremely sad one. And it seemed to me therefore that his speech, the occasion, the ceremony, and so on, seemed to be completely in keeping with the contents of the agreement, which themselves also make the Palestinians subordinate dependents of the Israelis, who will in fact continue to control the West Bank and Gaza for the foreseeable future.

In your most recent book, *Culture and Imperialism*, the major themes of superior/subordinate relationships, colonialism, racism, and imperialism are refracted through the prism of literature. I sense a lot of those issues echoing in the South Lawn on that bright Monday morning as well.

The key to it, from my point of view, and something that in effect caused me to resign from the Palestine National Council (PNC) in the late summer/early fall of 1991, was the sense in which the PLO, having once been a fighting organization, or at least an organization that represented the spirit of the Palestinians fighting, not to kill Jews, but for rights, for freedom, equality, had, by entering the

Madrid process, in fact subordinated itself to the U.S. and Israel. That was what was so disturbing about the ceremony.

It was in many ways for Arafat his greatest moment. He has since told people, and it's appeared in the Arabic press, saying, Do you realize what it means to be invited to the White House? And so on. So there's a sense of a kind of "nigger mentality," the white man's nigger, that we are finally arrived and they've patted us on the head and we've been accepted and can sit on their nice chairs and talk to them. But at the same time to many Palestinians, I don't mean the ones who have been in the streets in Jericho and Gaza, whom he may have paid to demonstrate, I'm not sure, it was an act of surprising indignity and permanent subordination, as if the U.S. holds the key to all our future, whereas there's a complete amnesia when it comes to what the U.S. has done to our people since 1948. And as recently as in the last year.

Don't forget that during the period of the secret negotiations—which actually didn't begin in Oslo but began in the fall of 1992 between some high PLO officials and a few paid Palestinian consultants and a few Israel security experts negotiating in Boston at the American Academy—they were negotiating future security arrangements for the West Bank and Gaza, mainly security for Israeli citizens. Nobody ever said anything about security for Palestinians.

So that's where it began. During that period, from October until September of this year, this was the worst period of oppression on the West Bank. More people were killed in the early part of the year, twenty or thirty people in Gaza, a lot of them children under fifteen. This was the time of the deportations. In December, Israel deported 415 Palestinians, claiming they were all terrorists, and just threw them out on the Lebanese border. This was the time of the closure of the territories, not just the closure, but also when I was there you could see that they had put barricades up on all the roads. Israel controls all the roads. So circulation within the occupied territories became very difficult. And it was during this period that they were negotiating a secret agreement which said nothing about any of these things and therefore the expulsion, for example, was never mentioned, and above all the 14,000 or 15,000 political prisoners never came up.

So it's an astonishing feat of national self-obliteration that was performed by Arafat and the appalling way he said at the end of this speech, "Thank you, thank you, thank you." Thanking the U.S. for what? Thanking Israel for what? A mere month and a half before that Israel had invaded Lebanon and publicly declared that it was trying to create, and indeed did create, somewhere between 400,000 and 500,000 refugees in southern Lebanon. None of this was mentioned. So it's a matter of some concern to us.

You've had a sense of foreboding for quite some time, even before your resignation from the Palestine National Council. You were quoted in an interview in the late 1980s as saying that the PLO, the movement is "dominated by class interests that are not at all progressive. There is a tremendous confluence of the high Palestinian bourgeoisie in the PLO" and, as you just alluded to, "with an ideological dependency on the U.S."

I actually had been saying these things at least ten years before. I spent the summer of 1979 in Beirut, and there I gave a series of lectures and seminars on the relationship between the Arab world and the U.S. In one of the public lectures I gave I was asked about the question of negotiations. I said that I had no doubt that the PLO was going to negotiate with Israel. That isn't what worries me. What worries me is what sort of negotiations are they going to be, towards what end these negotiations are going to be taking place, and what kind of independence and above all what kind of Palestinian state are we talking about. There my fears were, if I could say so about myself, quite prescient, because I was already worried that they would be in fact the interests not of the large mass of Palestinians, who are basically impoverished or stateless and certainly landless. But really they would serve the interests of what was increasingly the upper echelons of the PLO, that is to say, bourgeois, ideologically dependent on the U.S. and capitalism, no serious interest in reforming not only the structure of Palestinian society, but the Arab world of which we were a part. And that's why we had so many adherents in the Arab world. It wasn't because we were trying to take a piece of land, but because we represented a secular struggle towards freedom and democracy and above all social and ideological transformation. This never happened.

To what extent do you think Arafat and the people around him have internalized racist and colonialist attitudes?

I don't really know about that. It's hard for me to penetrate the psychology of people I don't see very often. But I certainly felt that there was a qualitative change in the Palestinian leadership and the PLO's leadership after 1982, after the disaster of the Lebanese invasion by Israel and the fact that the Palestinian leadership was forced to leave Lebanon at the behest and with the cooperation of the U.S. and to sit in Tunis. During the decade of the 1980s the Palestinian leadership in Tunis lost touch with its people, and I think with its mission. I paid frequent visits there, and I was always incredibly disappointed after I left.

I still believe that the PLO is the only institution we have. It's not owned by Arafat and the few people who have been left to surround him, basically sycophants and mercenaries and people of that sort, but it's a national institution. But during the decade of the 1980s I noticed in fact that the popular sense of what the PLO was, was almost always risible. People used to laugh at Arafat and his posturing. I think obviously they were taken by surprise by the intifada, although they worked with it. The single great achievement of that decade was the PNC meeting of 1988 in Algiers. But that was in a certain sense forced on the PLO by events on the ground and by the astonishing success of this mass anti-colonial insurrection which was the intifada.

But I think the final decline set in with the Gulf War. They were isolated, with a tremendous sense of fantasy. I recall even in December of 1990 top leaders of the PLO were in New York and they were telling me at the same time, a) that there's not going to be a war, when it was clear to anybody who lived in this country that there was going to be a war, and b) if there was a war, Iraq would certainly win. This person, number two or three in the organization, told me, Iraq has weapons that you've never heard of. They're going to destroy the U.S. So this was essentially the tactical, strategic, ideological blunder of supporting a government and being supported by a government such as that of Saddam Hussein's. I felt from then on that there was no remedying the situation, principally because there was no accountability, no mechanism for accountability.

After 1990, as my friend Shafiq al-Hout became a member of the Executive Committee in 1991, partly due to the efforts of Mahmoud Darwish and myself, it was noted that Arafat had sole control over the money. Nobody could sign a check except he. He was the only person who knew where the money had gone. And when his plane crashed in Libya in the spring of 1992, this had caused consternation because people said, Who's going to pay our salary now? Because he was the only man who knew where the money was.

So I think all that created an ideological paralysis that in my opinion was ripe for a sudden, dramatic, and even theatrical quick solution, which in the end was really a solution just to assure the survival of the traditional leadership of the PLO.

In terms of cultural stereotypes as they are alive and thriving in the Middle East, this whole notion of back-channel negotiations I think plays into that.

Yes. The stereotype now on the side of the Palestinians, which I have been very involved in, this is really my main, I wouldn't call it "struggle," because that would perhaps be dignifying it too much, but my efforts with regard to the PLO leadership were to try to explain to them the way the U.S. works, and that the worst thing we could do would be to do what in fact they did during the Reagan and Bush period, namely, and that's why Madrid went through, was to try to rely on and ally ourselves exclusively with the power of the day. In this case it was the president and that particular administration, in the completely misguided hope that some important person, usually a man, would be able to deliver a solution if you got close enough to him, if you promised him things, if you were able to show that you would act later on in his interests. I tried to explain to them that the U.S. wasn't like Syria. It isn't as if you found Hafez al-Assad or an assistant to him or a minister who was on your side then you could unlock the doors, that the U.S. was a complex society, that there was the establishment, which was and still is completely opposed to the aspirations of Palestinian self-determination, their social and political message. There were the media, the universities, the churches, the minorities, the ethnic groups, the associations, the labor movement. All these things, I've been saying this since the late 1970s, should be attended to. But they couldn't because their stereotype was that if you find a white man who's prominent, he'll be able to deliver the whole thing. This infected even the negotiations and the delegation, who should have known better.

I'll give you an example. In the spring of 1992, in April, in the middle of the presidential primaries, an Arab friend of mine in Washington found out that at that time candidate Clinton was in Washington and staying very close to if not actually in the same hotel as the Palestinian delegation, which was in negotiations with the Israelis. This friend of mine went to the Clinton people and said, Look, I would like Governor Clinton to meet members of the Palestinian delegation. And Clinton said, Yes, I'd be delighted to. He was looking around for support. He still hadn't made his commitment as strongly as he later did to Israel. So this friend of mine went to the Palestinian delegation, and they refused. He said to them, Why not? They said, We don't want to do this, because if the Republicans and the Bush Administration found out that we made contact with the Democratic contender, they'd be very upset and we wouldn't get anywhere. So they didn't. Even after the election in November, there was a round in December 1992 in Washington, Clinton had already been elected, they still were very unhappy about the prospects of meeting with a Democrat, because they were afraid that Baker might still deliver something to them in the last month of the administration.

Whereas in fact the Bush Administration, which the Palestinians supported publicly, had already delivered the $10 billion loan guarantees to Israel, had approved or at least didn't demur enough at the deportation of the Palestinians in December 1992. All of this is an ideological stereotype, not by Americans about Palestinians, those are bad enough. This stereotype is by Palestinians about Americans.

It was extraordinarily stupid and ignorant.

There's no excuse for ignorance. We're not talking about Palestinians who live in the U.S. Leaving aside the top leaders, Arafat knows nothing about the West, has never lived in it. Mahmoud Abbas, the man who signed the agreement, doesn't even know English. Arafat can't read and write English with any technical skill at all. But I'm talking about the advisors. Many of them have been educated in America and remain as ideologically hobbled as Arafat and his advisors. That's the real tragedy. It's the intellectuals, the people who have been educated in this country, who haven't really used their knowledge to transform the consciousness so that at least we might have the hope of dealing with the U.S. from a position of equality with some understanding of what the U.S. is as a system, not as a bunch of individuals whom we may like or not like.

There seems to me a certain, I hate to use such a charged term, tribalism at work here, with the *zaeem* at top, the clan leader, the chief, who is unquestioned.

I'm not sure I would use that. Tribalism is a vaguely racist idea. It's not that. I think it really is a social, political, and ideological choice that in times of crisis your idea of your own national movement, which has, alas, to its discredit, perpetuated this sort of notion, continues to hold onto a style of politics which is not progressive, a style of politics that's authoritarian, and that can exist in developed countries as well. You see it in many parts of Europe, the return of authoritarianism. What you call tribalism I call xenophobia. The idea that no matter what Palestinians do they're right, just because they're Palestinians. The leadership has to be supported. In our movement, there's a lot of talk about democracy. Relative to the Arab world there is democracy. People can speak. I always spoke quite loudly and critically. But the idea of an institutional opposition doesn't exist. The idea is that somehow you have to support the leader, and the leader knows best. The tragedy is that some of these intellectuals in the movement, who a week before this secret agreement was revealed on August 27 were crying to me about how terrible the situation inside the PLO had become, how unreachable Arafat had become, how autocratic, how he was surrounded by lackeys, the circle had shrunk. Twenty-four hours after the agreement was signed, they turned around and became supporters of Arafat as a great genius and what a wonderful thing had happened, as if politics is the politics of secret deals, great leaders, and suddenly transformative events, like miracles, a kind of theological view of politics. That's the problem.

What are the details of the accord and their ramifications?

The general view now is that it's a done deal.

It's being celebrated by Americans across the board. Many liberal Jews, friends of Peace Now, critics of the Likud in America, are also celebrating it. I think there's a sense in which even for Palestinians who are dismayed by the actual agreement, there's a sense in which they concur, and to a certain degree I do also, in saying, let's hope that it leads to something better. Because I don't think anybody is fooled; it's clear this is an agreement between vastly unequal parties. Yet one of the most extraordinary statements was made by Nabil Shaath, the spokesman for Arafat, who had nothing to do with the deal; he was here when it was struck. On television he said that this is a declaration of principles that establishes absolute "parity" between the Israelis and the Palestinians. Such nonsense I don't think has fooled anybody. Certainly no Palestinian I know believes it. But there's a sense in which, for example, among Palestinians on the West Bank and Gaza, with whom I've spoken constantly since I returned from there, almost on a daily basis, that at least there's a chance that the Israelis will withdraw from some sections. The fatigue of twenty-six years of brutal military occupation, and the expectation that there might be slightly more freedom, that there might be more money coming in, that things might improve towards independence, is shared by everyone, including myself. But I don't feel that we can move forward realistically without really understanding what the agreement says and what it doesn't say.

So I think the first thing to understand, therefore, is that it's really a direct reflection of our weakness as the second party with Israel. So that has to be acknowledged. And in it are the terms of the victor. So we have to understand it as an instrument of capitulation on a lot of major points. It provides Palestinians with some relative degree of improvement, but also tremendous restrictions, many of which are now given a kind of legalistic expression which we have signed and accepted, at least the leadership has accepted it. You can't move forward until you can understand what's in it. You can't say, Let's see if we can make it work until we know what in it is there to be made to work and what isn't.

The first big thing to understand is the effects of accepting an interim solution, which is what this is declared to be, a declaration of principles on interim phase settlement. We have a claim to the occupied territories, which we and the world generally, including the U.S., have always regarded as the occupied territories, therefore to be vacated, liberated from occupation. This agreement puts them on the same level as disputed territories. Israel in effect has said, and we have accepted, let's not talk about sovereignty, which is the principal issue here, or control. Let's talk about autonomy and limited self-rule in the interim period, leaving questions of the settlements, of sovereignty, of land, of water, of Jerusalem, and so on, to what are called final status negotiations, where the Palestinians will advance their claim and the Israelis will advance their claim as equals. The claims are equal, not the parties. In the meantime, Israel controls the land.

I think it is very important to understand that we have sacrificed what we have through our own struggle in the international arena for years and in the Arab world gained, namely the notion that these are occupied territories and not administered territories. Israel to this day, and certainly not in the agreement, does not regard itself as a military occupier. There's nothing in the agreement that says that Israel is going to withdraw finally. It says that there is going to be withdrawal from some areas, redeployment of troops in others. The settlements and all the other things are going to remain. So it has to be understood, that Israel will control, as Rabin said in a press conference the day of the ceremony, access to and passage across the Jordan River, the sea, the Gaza Coast, the international boundaries between Gaza and Egypt and between Jordan and Jericho. It will control the land between Gaza and Jericho, which is about ninety kilometers, about sixty miles. And it will control security as well as foreign affairs.

Rabin implied in his press conference that the PLO should stop spending money on its embassies, of which there are now almost a hundred, and put that money into Gaza. Indeed, in the last six or eight months, many PLO embassies, including those in London, Paris, Holland, New York, and elsewhere, have not been receiving money from the PLO. The claim has been that the PLO is bankrupt. Salaries haven't been paid, etc. I see that as an ominous sign that many international embassies of the PLO, including its representation to international organizations like the UN, are going to be closed down.

The PLO is in fact, and this is the second major point, has now become not only a signatory to this declaration of principle but in fact a municipal government. The Israeli rhetoric is very careful and precise. They never said that the PLO is anything more than a political party. It's not a national party. It's not the national representative of a nation. It is not the expression of Palestinian self-determination. It is a local party, like the Likud, like Labor, which contends with these others for a certain amount of control. So there's an inclusion there.

Third, is the issue of development. Although the Palestinians will have relative control over such things as tourism, health, sanitation, direct taxation, etc., when it comes to development, the main premise of this agreement has been that there will suddenly be, for the first time, a massive influx of funds. Israel and the Palestinians together will form what is called a development council. But Israel has a much stronger economy that has penetrated the West Bank and Gaza, so much so that 85 percent of the economy of the West Bank and Gaza is dependent on Israel, Israeli manufacturing, etc., or controlled by it. This will also give Israel control over development funds that will come in. So Israeli projects and economic concerns on the West Bank and Gaza have to be served along with Palestinian ones. So that when people are talking now about huge World Bank projects, European Community projects, Arab state projects, there's a tendency to forget that Israel is involved in that, too.

I think this aspect of development is perhaps the most dangerous. It's quite clear that with this agreement Israel recaptures officially the Palestinian markets of the West Bank and Gaza, which are to it simply a place for exports, for cheap wage labor, which will continue to work under those conditions. Perhaps with the Palestinian bourgeoisie, the entrepreneurial class will develop certain things that have nothing to do with the well being of the people, like resorts and hotels, and so on. These are the first projects being talked about. The infrastructure will be, in a sense, controlled by the Israelis, along with, but less so, by the Palestinians. This will also provide a springboard for Israel into the rest of the Arab world. Palestine will become a bridge for the dynamic Israeli economy, which is much more organized and much more powerful because of its relationship with the U.S. and the West, as an entree into the Arab world, which is what it has always wanted.

These are all extraordinary disabilities of the accord. A fourth point: one has to remember that throughout all this period, Israel's army will remain, the settlements will remain. What this means, for example, in Gaza is that approximately 40 percent of Gaza has been taken by the settlements and the army. So the withdrawal will not give Palestinians control of Gaza, which is the phrase that's been used, but will give it relative autonomy of its part of Gaza, which they have to control, and worst of all, that they will in fact do the job for Israel of enforcing law and order, as the Israelis have not been able to do. As Rabin said in his press conference, the Palestinians are responsible for the security not just of the Palestinian citizens of Gaza, but of the Israelis who are there as well. They have to pass through Palestinians' territories, admittedly escorted by Israeli soldiers, which will remain.

The question then is, What about the right to resist? Since the Gaza strip is still under military occupation, let's say a child throws a stone at a jeep. Who is going to prosecute that child? Nothing has been said about the political prisoners. What happens if Palestinians arrest this child for throwing stones? Will he be put in an Israeli prison or into a Palestinian prison administered by the Israelis? These are extraordinary questions which, for example, other liberation movements have avoided. For example, the ANC (African National Congress), even though it won a victory, and of course we didn't win a victory, refused to participate in a police force until they were in government, until they had control of the government. We have accepted this role beforehand.

A couple of weeks ago there was an item in the Arabic press where about two hundred Palestinians from the Palestine Liberation Army, of which some of the members have been trained for police duty in Gaza and Jericho, refused to go because they said, We don't want to become the policemen of Israel, which is the perception that most people now have of the PLO. It's going to be an enforcer for Israel. So the question of the right to resist, which for me and indeed international law gives us that right, has now been compromised by the PLO's deal.

A final point is that the PLO is going to be in conflict with local authorities. Don't forget that all of the people in the PLO that we have been talking about, including Arafat and his top people, have never been on the West Bank. They know nothing about it. And the struggle, the horrors of occupation have been lived by people who have achieved a status, for example, in their communities, who through sacrifice and ingenuity and resourcefulness have survived in their own way. They're going to find it very hard to cede authority to the PLO that comes in from the outside with its own policemen. So there is I think a built-in situation that might lead to a kind of civil, I wouldn't call it war, but civil strife.

That strife has already begun. And it's not entirely a matter of the PLO versus Hamas and the Islamic movements in the West Bank and Gaza. I think those have been grossly overestimated by the Western media and policymakers for other reasons. But I think that the Palestinians themselves are not going to be happy about the methods of the PLO. Don't forget that twice in the last couple of months Arafat has publicly answered to Israeli and Arab interviewers who asked him, What is your background in government, you are a liberation organization leader? He said, I controlled Beirut for ten years. If you tell that to a Lebanese, or even a Palestinian who lived in Beirut during that time, that's not a very happy thing to remember, and it doesn't provide a very interesting model.

What about the control of water under this agreement? Meron Benvenisti, the former Israeli deputy mayor of Jerusalem, says that up to eighty percent of the West Bank aquifer is being taken by Israel, not only for its settlements but actually water is also going into pre-1967 Israel.

Water is obviously the clue, but it's one among many clues which have to do first with preemptive control by Israel, which now controls them. That's number one. As you said, every significant aquifer in the West Bank has been tapped into by Israel. They are using it not only for the watering of the settlements, but also they take it into Israel. There are probably works underground that we know nothing about in south Lebanon, near the Litani, and there have been attempts over the past twenty-five years to divert and tap into the Jordan River, the tributaries of the Jordan. So there's a system in operation here for which no Arab state, and certainly not the Palestinians, has anything comparable. The same is true of land. Nobody really knows what land Israel has taken, what land is already designated as expropriated for military purposes and what land is already taken by the settlements. If you look at Jerusalem, if you go and see Jerusalem, Greater Jerusalem now is approximately 25 or 30 percent of the West Bank. There's nothing in the agreement that says they're going to give back Jerusalem, because that's been postponed until the final status, without any mechanism for getting from the interim to the final status negotiations. So that's one problem.

The second point connected to water and land is in my opinion a much more debilitating one. At least on the first point you can fight: you can say, You have done this and this. But the much more debilitating point is that the Palestinians to this stage don't have the requisite amounts of information about what Israel has done. This is characteristic throughout the Arab world, it's a general problem, that people don't really know because the state doesn't publish statistics that are reliable. Everything is governed by ideology and political control. You never really know what in fact is taking place. You could see in the secret agreement that a lot of it was done purposely to screen off the majority of a fairly aware population of Palestinians from complaining or worrying about the situation. This produces levels of incompetence. This agreement was negotiated in English by people who don't know English, and without a lawyer. So, for example in the case of water, we don't have an adequate picture of what the water situation is. We don't know enough about what Israel has taken of the land. I spoke to Nabil Shaath by phone after the agreement was announced in Washington. I told him, The Israelis have already taken over fifty percent of the land. He said, No, in the negotiations we discovered that they'd only taken two or three percent. I said, That's simply not true.

So the playing with information for a personal or political advantage is very much part of the scene. There's no sense in which independents, such as myself or Chomsky or others, have any authority over a movement that has decided this is a great victory and we've won and it's parity. Shaath and Arafat have said this is a great moment and we've been accepted by the White House. Details like land and water come much, much later, when people wake up and when we develop the expertise necessary to find out what is at stake. In the meantime the settlements continue to expand. It's much more ominous than just that they took the land. We don't even know how much they took, and where they took it, and what they've done to the water, which is already plugged into the Israeli system. It's not as if you can take out a tap from there and put it somewhere else. It's already a working part of the system.

And, I'm afraid, the accord is a very inadequate response to the realities.

About Gaza: There have been some remarkable admissions in the mainstream media describing it as it is, an incredibly impoverished place that has no infrastructure. There's extensive poverty, open sewers, etc. But at the same time while reporting on these things and the need for massive amounts of money, there is no commentary on what has been

going on in Gaza in twenty-six years of Israeli occupation, in terms of providing services, clinics, roads, schools, and the like.

Gaza, first of all, is made up largely of refugees.

One has to understand that about 80 percent of the people that now inhabit Gaza, roughly 900,000, just a hair under a million people, are not from Gaza. They are people from the north, who have come from Haifa and Jaffa. In other words, they are 1948 refugees who are stuck in refugee camps like Jabalya, which has 65,000 people, or squatters throughout the area or people who live in homeless and desperate conditions, in an extraordinarily constricted space. If you look at the settlements, they breathe an air of luxury. They live in Gaza, therefore, about 90 percent of the people in absolute poverty, with no infrastructural change or development in the twenty-six years of Israeli occupation.

Don't forget that in 1971–72 Ariel Sharon was personally in charge of the pacification of Gaza. Gaza was always insurrectionary, for various reasons. Large new settlements were built. People were moved around. The massive plan for Gaza was such that Israeli control, which has never been very successful, could be instituted from Gaza. You wouldn't have to bring troops from outside through the settlements and permanent military installations in Gaza. That's one major point.

The second major point about Gaza is that the Israelis have always wanted to get rid of it. So they have never put much money into it. Look at the figures that Rabin used in his press conference, which I thought was much more interesting than anything he said in public otherwise, Rabin went on about the $350 million a year that they've spent on the West Bank and Gaza. But if you look at the actual condition of life in Gaza, with open sewers, the absence of electricity, the total lack of any sanitation or garbage removal, and above all the lack of work, since the Gaza economy is totally dependent on people going as day laborers into Israel proper, you'll see that Gaza has been standing still. It has become one of the most squalid and poorest spots on earth.

But, more important than that, is that Gaza also is a place where there's a great deal of wealth. There's a huge disparity between the top families. Gaza, like many parts of Palestine, is characterized by having a few large landed families who own property in Gaza and who live lives that are completely out of touch with the condition of peasants and day laborers and refugees who are the majority of the population. There is a social problem of some importance. Because of this, Gaza is a place where the most radical ideological, whether Islamic or non-Islamic, the Popular Front, the Communist Party, Hamas, are very powerful. They address social issues in Gaza, not just the occupation but also the internal situation.

None of this has been covered by the press. One gets the impression that Gaza is a place where Palestinians live and the Israelis have given away in an act of noblesse oblige, and so forth, without the realization that Gaza has always been an albatross around their neck. As recently as six months ago both Rabin and Peres said, We wish Gaza would go away, drop in the sea. Those phrases have been used. Gaza is the place where the intifada began, where the most casualties of children have occurred. It has the largest population of individuals under the age of fifteen, who account for over 60 percent of the population. So in all this, to talk about infrastructural reform in Gaza is a noble idea, but what I fear is that Gaza is going to become, because Israel controls the port, either a large pool of unorganized, cheap labor, selling services to the Israelis, or it's going to become a center of semiskilled industry which will be on the border like some of the Mexican towns like Tijuana, supplying southern California with laborers and house servants, or through the assembly plants and small factories, cheap labor for that, which is very alarming. When I was there in early July of '93, there had been a great deal of land speculation, even before the accord was announced, as there has been in Jericho. People have known about this possibility, it's been spoken about since the middle of the spring of this year. So there's been a lot of land speculation. Land speculation means not building of houses for refugees, but things like resorts, hotels, tourist centers, and so on. The situation in Gaza is likely to develop in an extraordinarily unhappy way, I think.

I know music is a very important part of your being and who you are. I see a kind of metaphor here in terms of what has evolved. You've always said that you've loved music where voices respond to each other, echoing each other, contrasting each other, a kind of horizontal line as opposed to a vertical line represented by monophonic music. Is this a metaphor for what's happened in these negotiations, in terms of the lack of those voices?

I wouldn't say that, because the counterpoint is quite clear. This is why I was so critical of the accord. Israel really needed a Palestinian partner in order to produce a settlement that it can live with comfortably, that could be a wonderful deal, not just for its relations with the Palestinians, but also for its relations with the other Arabs and above all for its public image, which had sunk to very new lows because of the intifada, the invasion of Lebanon in July of 1993, etc. That's why I blame the PLO leadership for what they did. They knew that their main card was to be the Israeli's other voice. Instead of assessing that and understanding that there could be no peace with Palestinians without the PLO, Arafat, in order to serve himself at a particularly low moment in his career, sacrificed the one card he had left to play to Israel, to give them a credible Palestinian interlocutor, what the French in Algeria were always looking for, what the FLN refused to give them, an *interlocuteur relable*. The PLO did this, with the occupation still on, with the destruction of the intifada, with the PLO in its weakest moment.

It was a brilliantly struck deal by the Israelis, and they could therefore say, We have a partner. But the partner is kind of a mimic of themselves. It's not a real partner, a partner that represents the aspirations and hopes of the Palestinian people. It's in fact a party that has shed itself of its own history and its own representativity. So there is a main burden for us now, Palestinians who are in the diaspora, which produced the PLO. The PLO is not a creation of the West Bank and Gaza, which have been under occupation. It's a creation of the diaspora. So the main topic for us today, as the three million people, over half the population on whom the PLO is going to have to depend as it tries to develop its autonomy into something better than the present situation or even the present agreement allows, is more democracy. The main hope that we have is to reorganize ourselves and to begin to demand from the PLO as our representative more representation, more democracy, to make sure, for example, that the elections, which are supposed to take place in the next six to nine months, in fact do take place. To make sure they take place despite the fact that many Israeli commentators are saying that the secret agreement between Rabin and Arafat has been not to have elections, to postpone the elections so that the PLO can continue to rule. We have to make sure of elections. And we have to make sure that there's an accountability. We can't have leaders who say, I know best and I'm going to do it. If we want to participate, the price for participation has to be full participation, not just giving money and support and public declarations of good feeling, but actually getting involved in this. I think that's the major problem.

One point I want to mention which is extraordinarily important, it seems silly and trivial but it has been the case for many years, is that there is no Palestinian census. For the last ten years some of us have been trying to say, The thing that we need to know in order to give our political empowerment greater profile is to say who and where we are. The Arab states have always opposed a census. They don't want to know. They don't want a public counting of Palestinians, nor do the Israelis. I think now the major demand should be, and I'm making this public, as have many others, is that we want a Palestinian census in every country where a Palestinian resides in order for there to be assemblies of Palestinians. Our problem is dispersion and representation. You can't have that unless you're identified as a Palestinian who has a direct stake in the continuing existence of Palestinian life on Palestinian soil. To this end therefore I think it's terribly important that questions of elections, of representative institutions on the West Bank and elsewhere be tied to the question of a census and not just be left as, Let's have an election and make sure that our guys win. That's not the idea. In other words, the period of nationalism has to end, and we now have to enter a new period of social and political transformation, which takes us to another level where people are involved, where people are mobilized and not just left to the whims of the leader.

To this day, Arafat has not publicly explained his position to the people as it really is. I believe he should have. He should have said, Because of my mistakes, because of our misjudgments in the Gulf War, this is the only alternative that we have. I must ask you, Do you accept it? If you do, we will sign it. If not, I will remove myself. He didn't do that. Abdel Nasser did that in June 1967. He hasn't explained to his people why he turned down so many alternatives in the past. Some of them I was involved in. He could have gotten much better deals from the Americans and the Israelis in the 1970s and the 1980s, but he turned them all down. So why was he saving himself up for this particular deal? That's a question that needs to be answered. It hasn't been answered.

Sol Linowitz, one of the Carter Camp David negotiators, was on a *MacNeil/Lehrer* celebration one night with the usual suspects: Kissinger, Brzezinski, and Brent Scowcroft. Linowitz said, It's really sad, while he was very happy, because the Palestinians could have gotten all of this and more at Camp David in 1979. I wonder how much of that is historical engineering?

It's true. I don't know about Camp David. In the fall of 1978, and I'm saying this publicly for the first time, through Hodding Carter, a classmate of mine who was working in the Carter Administration, I saw Secretary of State Vance in New York more than once. We discussed it. He said that he didn't want to be talking with me. He wanted to be talking with Arafat. I said it could be arranged. He said, No, there are rules, and my predecessor—he never referred to Kissinger except as "my predecessor"—we are forbidden to talk to the PLO. He said, We have a formula which I'd like you to take to Chairman Arafat. The formula was that the PLO accept 242 with the reservation, since 242 doesn't talk about Palestinians, that the rights of the Palestinian people to national self-determination are still its goal. The U.S. would then recognize the PLO and begin to negotiate with Arafat directly, and then institute negotiations with Israel.

I thought it was a good idea. I sent a message with Shafiq al-Hout, who was in New York for the UN, directly to Arafat. I waited for weeks and never heard back. Then Vance called me in the early part of 1979 just before they actually signed the Camp David accord and said, I'd like to know what the answer of Chairman Arafat is. I said, I haven't heard from him. He said, I will dictate the text to you again to make sure that it fits all the criteria. So in March of 1979 I flew to Beirut and went to see Arafat. I said to him, We need an answer. The first thing he said was, I never received the message. So for at least ten minutes he began to deny that any message came. Luckily, Shafiq al-Hout was sitting with us in the room and he said, I delivered the message to you. Arafat said, I have no recollection of it. Shafiq went into the next room and brought a copy of it. Arafat looked at it and said, All right, tomorrow I'll give you my answer. The next day he came back with about fifteen of his lieutenants, including Abu Jihad and Abu Iyyad, the *etat major* (general staff) of the Palestinian people. They came in. He sat down. He said, Edward, I want you to tell Vance that we're not interested. I said, Why? He said, We don't want the Americans. The Americans have stabbed us in the back. This is a lousy deal. We want Palestine. We're not interested in bits of Palestine. We don't want to negotiate with the Israelis. We're going to fight.

This was in 1979. There were many such deals that went on through the 1980s as he got weaker and weaker. He had no troops to command. It was clear to me, at any rate, in the 1970s that we had no military option against Israel, any more than they had against us, but he turned it down. These are part of the historical record, and they need to be known. I think these have to be asked of the Palestinian leadership now, when it's trying to avoid questions, trying to go forward in a great march toward whatever it is that they call it. These questions have to be asked so that we know where we're going.

I'm not saying that we should be like King Canute and say that the agreement has to be withdrawn. But we have to know what's in the agreement, where it came from, and where it's possible to go.

Let's talk about the media and their whole spin on this. There is an almost unanimous chorus of euphoria in the U.S. What about the European media that you monitor? Any difference there?

I've done a lot of interviews in the European media where I've expressed my reservations, and that's gotten more interest. People are beginning to ask questions. There's an attempt to get below the surface. In America, I'm sorry to say, with the exception of a few outlets and a few individuals, and I think the individuals are the ones who make the difference, the media have been extraordinary. A matter of a month ago Arafat was probably the most reviled man in the world. He was considered a terrorist. There wasn't a single interview in which he didn't appear badly. The questions were always, Why are you a terrorist? The only thought ascribed to him was that he was planning the murder of innocent Jewish children and women. In a matter of a few hours he was rehabilitated. He turned into a lovable figure. The Americans loved him. They said he was a statesman. I understand that when he went to Congress, Senators Dole and Mitchell, among others, were standing in line to get his autograph. This kind of shameless about-face puts to rest, if it needed to be put to rest, the myth of the independent media.

The media exist mainly as a gloss on American power and policy. Although there have been many stories on how the U.S. was taken by surprise in this development, what hasn't been noticed is that the differences between this development and what the U.S. has always wanted are cosmetic. Even if it wasn't Aaron David Miller and Dennis Ross and Dan Kurzer and Edward Djerejian and Warren Christopher who in fact engineered it, what in fact emerged was something that they couldn't be unhappy with. It gives, in effect, a U.S. surrogate, Israel, enormous regional power. It's become a regional superpower control. Finally, as Christopher and Baker both said, this is the defeat of Arab radicalism and Arab nationalism. So this is an agreement that puts the U.S. back in the driver's seat, gives it superpower status yet again, and allows it to use this agreement to assure its opening towards the markets and resources of the Gulf, for which Palestine is an important entrance.

The media have simply not performed. They have just been another, in my opinion, stupid chorus in its selection of voices and spokesmen and so forth, and alas, and I say this with great shame and unhappiness, the Palestinians reproduced exactly the right kinds of spokesmen to be a part of this chorus, people who in the past were Fanonists a matter of a week ago and have now changed and become advocates of Singapore and open markets and development. They do nothing for the real mass of the Palestinians, who are landless peasants, stateless refugees, cheap wage earners at slave labor, and this preserves the hegemony of the traditional families and the traditional leadership.

So I think the media are enormously powerful.

CNN has an incredible reach. But in terms of informing, it doesn't. It simply confirms the world ideological system, now controlled, I believe, by the U.S. and a few allies in Western Europe.

Let's say you're an average person on a beach. You're about to be engulfed in a tidal wave of information and disinformation. How do you stay dry? How do you cut through the webs of media deceit?

There are two faculties that we all possess and have to exercise in a situation like this, when there's a media blitz, as there is most of the time when one story is the issue. They are: number one, memory. We have to remember what they said the day before, which is often exactly the opposite. The second faculty is skepticism. The one comes from actually experiencing these things. If you remember as a television watcher, an American, you saw Arafat reviled as a terrorist and all of a sudden he seems like a nice guy just because he utters a few words, you know something is wrong. It can't happen that quickly. Second of all, the skepticism is part of your intellectual and critical faculty. It seems to me you have to do that with any news item. To try to ask more than what is presented in the twenty-two minutes that are now legitimated as the "news hour" on television. I think anybody can do this. There are always alternative sources of information. There are books, libraries. You just have to exercise those skills and refuse to allow yourself to become a vegetable that simply absorbs information, prepackaged, pre-ideologized, because no message on television is anything but an ideological package that has gone through a kind of processing process.

There's also the blinding power of the klieg lights and the power of the image.

That's where I find it most disappointing to see other intellectuals completely taken up with that. I've never found it interesting to be close to power. I think power always needs the corrective of intellectual honesty and conscience and memory. The irony is so great that after the 1967 war, when the Palestinian movement emerged, we were famous in that movement for being critical. We were the first Arabs in our literature, our speeches, our writing, for example, to use the word "Israel." Everyone else talked about the "Zionist entity." We were the first ones to deal with reality. We criticized the Arab regimes that failed in 1967. Palestinian literature, scholarly and political analysis, was the first literature to use footnotes. We said we had to be responsible for what we said and that we were proceeding in an organized, disciplined, and intellectually honest way.

This is all gone now. Palestinian official literature is a chorus of approval for the leadership. We've become, in effect, what the other Arab regimes are. The tragedy of Arafat is that he is seeing himself not as a leader of a people. Although in his own personal style and the popularity he still enjoys he's still a simple man. He doesn't affect large cars and luxurious residences. He still lives very austerely. But he's seen himself as a leader who hobnobs with kings and presidents, and I think that loss of perspective, especially among intellectuals, has been the worst thing. The seductions of power. The delights of authority. The absence of dialogue. That, in theory, is what intellectuals should refute.

Gramsci, of whom you're very fond, has said he had a pessimism of the intellect and an optimism of the will. Does that inform your personal struggle?

Yes. They have to be linked causally. I say pessimism of the intellect first and then optimism of the will based on the pessimism of the intellect. In other words, you can't just say, Things are bad, but never mind, I'm going to go forward. You have to say things are bad, and analyze them intellectually. And on the basis of that analysis you construct a movement forward based on optimism, the ability and the desire and the wish to change things. But I find it's not the case here, where there's optimism right at the beginning of trying to turn, by magical process, what in effect is a disastrous agreement into a wonderful thing. They're saying it's parity, an opening, a foot in the door, it's going to change everything. That strikes me as irresponsible. That's not optimism of the will. That's magical thinking. Gramsci was very careful always to say that his work represented secular work and that these were parts of what he called the conquest of civil society. We haven't done the secular work yet. We have a long way to go. But I think it will happen. As Palestinians begin to rub their noses in the realities of this agreement and come up against the intransigence of the Israeli occupation, which is going to continue, they're going to understand that the only way forward is continued resistance.

You've said that, "What's been very important to me is the sense of a community and a movement in progress to which I am committed and in which I am implicated." What directions do you see yourself moving in now?

Mainly, I find myself for the first time in twenty-five years cut off from large numbers of the community who have felt for whatever reasons, most of them understandable, relief, a wish to be accepted, a wish to see an end in sight. I feel myself cut off from these people, these Palestinians, who are much happier than I am. So I am now a kind of a lonely voice. The important thing is to try to express my views as positively as possible and never just say, It's all bad, what a disaster. Or we shouldn't have done it. I've never said that. But to try to say, This is the situation and this is what we need to do in order to improve it. That's very hard to do alone. But I'm finding more and more people now as the euphoria lifts and as the celebration is over and as people have had a chance to think. People begin to realize that they have to rely on themselves. If their leaders have promised them things that they can't deliver, then they should ask them, Why have you done this?

You're looking for, as Eliot says, "those other echoes that inhabit the garden."

That's kind of mystical. But I think that what one needs is an awakening to the realities and the difficulties of the present situation. But if you can't do that, then as an intellectual you have to press on despite the marginalization and loneliness you feel.

PALESTINE: BETRAYAL OF HISTORY
FEBRUARY 17, 1994

David Barsamian: Since our last conversation in late September you have generated a series of interventions in various media around the world. There's been a steady trajectory in your critique of the PLO. That's culminated in your call for Arafat to resign. Why do you want the man who has represented the Palestinian cause for so long to step aside?

Edward Said: There are a number of reasons. It isn't so much directed at the man as the style and leadership he represents. He's a perfectly nice man, I'm sure. He was a good friend of mine for a long time. I admired his leadership. I think in a certain sense he's come to the end of any useful role that he can play. In the first place I think the events of the period roughly August 1990 until the present have really been a steady decline in the fortunes of the Palestinians. As leader of that decline, as the man responsible for it, although never made accountable for it, it seems to me the time has come for all of us to say, enough! He sacrificed the well-being of literally hundreds of thousands, if not millions, of Palestinians as a result of his position during the Gulf War. He entered a poorly considered, badly prepared-for public negotiation with Israel in Madrid the following year, in 1991. He led his people on the West Bank and Gaza misleadingly to negotiate with the Israelis on what in the end were honorable terms, all the while undermining them with his attempt to make a secret back-door deal with the Israelis. He finally concluded all of this with a disastrous and, in my opinion, completely illegal, not that we have all the means for legality, of course, but illegal within the framework of Palestinian civil society, such as it is, secret negotiation with Israel in Oslo. This sealed the fate of more than half the Palestinian population, those not resident on the West Bank and Gaza. They were excluded. He conceded everything to Israel's occupation on the basis of a very slender recognition by Israel of the representativity of the PLO, and nothing else. What he got in Gaza and Jericho is almost laughable, considering the sacrifices of the millions and generations of Palestinians who sacrificed their lives for the struggle. That's the general tone of the failure of that particular declaration of principles.

But beyond that, on the level of just technical competency, he had no legal advisors to help him. He doesn't know English. He negotiated with the Israelis in English. He concluded a deal that was so hastily put together that it left all the leverage in Israel's hands, which had all the leverage to begin with, i.e., the army, the settlements, the territories, the sovereignty, Jerusalem.

And since that time he's made matters worse by trying to retain control in his hands, continuing, in my opinion, to corrupt an entire people by methods of patronage, buying them off, playing people off against each other, all with the sole interest of not improving the Palestinian lot, which has actually gotten worse, but of keeping himself in power. Now he is actively seeking to co-opt more Palestinians to set up an economic authority of which he's the president, so that any aid that comes in he will control. He's quoted publicly in the Israeli press as saying, If I had $50 million I'd get out of my problems and there would be no opposition. He'd buy them off. His latest ploy is to set up a television and broadcasting authority on the West Bank, of which he, using a local figure, is the controller, saying that we're not ready for democracy yet. In effect, what he's going to set up is a mirror image of Radio Baghdad.

He's alienated anyone who isn't totally dependent on him for his or her livelihood, anybody of any competence and principles has left. I include people like Mahmoud Darwish and Shafiq al-Hout. The theme of Palestinian negotiations, such as they are, with Israel is not only a charade, they're a scandal in terms of disorganization. The PLO under his leadership has generated not a single fact about the realities of the occupation, which none of the people negotiating, like himself and Nabil Shaath, have ever actually seen with his own eyes. So they don't know what they're talking about when they talk about settlements and occupation.

The reality is a totally fractious, disintegrating community with no institutions at all left. There's no fighting force. There are no social institutions, no health institutions, no educational institutions. There are large and destitute populations of Palestinians in places like Gaza and Beirut and Damascus and Amman, unattended to. He is in sole control of the money. He is accountable to no one. He is the only one who can sign checks. He's the only person who knows where the checks are. Perhaps his wife now knows something. But his closest associates, like Abu Mazen and Yasir Abed Rabbo and one or two others, refuse to attend meetings with him anymore. Abu Mazen, I've been told recently, the man who signed the agreement in Washington with Peres on September 13, has said that he will not go to Jericho but has asked for political asylum in Morocco.

Given all of that, and I've barely scratched the surface, it's quite obvious that he can't continue.

For years you have been closely identified with the Palestinian cause, chief spokesperson in the U.S.

I didn't represent anyone. I was doing it on my own.

But you are the most visible figure in the media, particularly in the U.S. What you are describing must be more disconcerting to you.

It's extremely painful. When it comes to the public realm in the U.S., and in the West generally, it's very difficult now to stand up and talk about Palestinian rights when the popular perception, which has been very brilliantly manipulated by the Israelis and to a certain extent by the Clinton administration, is that the conflict has been settled. Palestinians are going to have a "state." The longstanding issues between us and the Israelis have been taken care of in a satisfactory and honorable way. After all, as you said, the leader of the Palestinian movement, Mr. Palestine himself, signed on the dotted line and said what a great thing it was. He's quoted today in the *New York Times* as expressing some disappointment in the Americans for not being as helpful as he had hoped they would be. This after he had said publicly on several occasions that he has a friend in the White House. Anybody with the slightest knowledge of U.S. policy and the realities of the U.S., all of which the Palestinian leadership has refused to have any direct knowledge of, just out of laziness and ignorance, could have told him that that's pure folly. The difficulty, of course, is when I'm asked to speak and write I'm in the strange position of not only being critical of the Israelis for their occupation policies but now also the Palestinians. There's also the problem that there's very little Palestinian activity in this country. Very few Palestinians speak up or are asked to speak up or can speak up. So one feels unhappy.

My first order of business isn't really to write so much in this country and in the West generally, but in Arabic. I write a column twice a month which is published widely in the Arab world.

Do you find that your ideas are widely debated?

I've gotten a tremendous amount of response.

People have asked me to come to the Middle East and play a more direct political role in centers of large Palestinian populations like Jordan and even Beirut. But I've refused. I'm not equipped to do that. My health forbids me to do it. I try the best I can at least to keep the debate going. What is most disheartening, however, is that a lot of intellectuals, and this I think can be laid directly at the door of the PLO leadership, are just laying back and waiting to see which way things are going to fall. There's an awful lot of money being promised. The European Community and the World Bank have promised millions. Vast sums are floated by people, usually middle-class intellectuals, who think of their families and bettering themselves. So there isn't, in other words, a concerted attempt made by Palestinian intellectuals, with a few exceptions, to mount a real offensive against the current policies, to try to change them and make a difference.

There's another problem, I wrote a column about it a month or so ago, that the degree of psychological penetration of Palestinian intellectual ranks by the Israelis is so great now that very few Palestinians have the capacity now to think independently. That is to say, there is this idea that we can only develop ourselves in collaboration with Israelis. This is at a time when the occupation has gotten worse. Israeli soldiers are killing Palestinians, destroying Palestinian homes, confiscating land, making life for Palestinians, especially in Gaza, a hell on earth. You have large numbers of intellectuals who do dialogues in public with the Israelis on the understanding that somehow this is going to improve our lot. Of course it hasn't. What it has done is to introduce a measure of capitulation, so that the will to resist is gone. That is the most important thing of all for me.

This intellectual colonialism that you just described is one of the themes of *Culture and Imperialism.*

It is the internalizing of the colonizer's perspective on you, that you are incapable of doing anything without his tutelage and without his support and that validation doesn't come from your own society and from your own values, but from his. It's so pernicious, so deep now that I wonder whether it can be stopped or changed. I don't want to heap all the problem in the lap of my people, but I think it's widespread in the Arab world. I think there's a sense of inevitability about the U.S., that it represents the winner. There is no deterrent. There is no alternative. It's no longer a bipolar world. There's only one pole. The U.S. sets the rules. It's invented this phrase "peace process," which is a barbarism in Arabic. A lot of people now of the intellectual community on the left who were part of the anti-imperialist resistance, Arab nationalists for decades have now switched and have become social scientists who speak a new language. That's quite extraordinary.

The main point to be made here is, going back to *Culture and Imperialism*, that the PLO, whose name is Palestinian Liberation Organization, which was born as a liberation movement, is I think the only liberation movement that I know of in the twentieth century that before independence, before the end of colonial occupation, turned itself into a collaborator with the occupying force. I know of no example of that switch. So in a certain sense, we've broken the pattern, which I suppose is a historical distinction of some sort.

I'm a little bit confused about some mixed signals that have been coming from two different sources. Shimon Peres was in Boston a couple of weeks ago. He was quoted as saying that Arafat had told him, "The PLO has decided that it will go for a confederation with Jordan, not a separate Palestinian state." Then a few days ago, the secretary general of Israel's ruling Labor Party said that the Palestinians would have their own independent state by the end of the decade.

I think there are two things to be said about that. Number one, when PLO leaders, including Arafat, make statements, they are statements of the moment. They have no preparation or study or careful strategic analysis and reasoning behind them. Therefore, in my opinion, they are somewhere between totally irresponsible and unimportant. It's true that there is a clause in one of the National Council resolutions that speaks about a confederation with Jordan. But from the beginning of the summer of last year until the present, with one or two exceptions largely forced upon the PLO by the Jordanians, the PLO has avoided any coordination with Jordan and has acted in a way to slight Jordan and Syria, which is quite foolish. There are obviously differences between Assad, Arafat, and Hussein.

Their constituencies are different. Their long-range interests are different and in many ways opposed to each other. But it's folly, given that there are large Palestinian populations in these countries, to completely ignore them and pretend that Arafat, who's now a frequenter of the great banquet tables of Paris and London, and his cohorts, to pretend that Palestine is some other place.

So I think his comments about confederation with Jordan was just paying lip service to this cause in the National Council and because he had been pulled out on the carpet by the Jordanians, who told him, You can't not deal with us. After all, we are your closest neighbor to the east. We have a large Palestinian population. The transiting point on the Allenby Bridge is the most important one for you. It's the closest to Jericho, if it ever gets anything resembling autonomy. So you can't do this. So that's one element.

The other is the Israeli position, which is many voices speaking many different things, partly in confusion, partly as a way of keeping the outside world in suspense and off balance. What Yossi Beilin says, for example, is very different from what Rabin says. What Peres says is very different from what Rabin says. There is a deliberate policy of mixed signals which I think ought to be understood only as that. The policies are on the ground. The fact is that in the last few months more Palestinian land was confiscated. In December alone they confiscated 9,000 *dunums*.

How large is a dunum?

It's four dunums to an acre. The settlement process is continuing. So any kind of Palestinian state or entity that's intended for the West Bank and Gaza is bound to be either controlled or partly annexed by

Israel. That's the way I would look at it. The Israelis who say, like the director general that you mentioned, that there's going to be a Palestinian state before the end of the decade, many Israelis have told me this, too. But my answer to that is, What kind of a state? Of course, I've never had any doubt that Palestinians would ultimately get self-determination. It's a long, torturous road. It doesn't go straight forward. There are lots of loops and bends and turns and backward motion. But what is at issue right now is the kind of polity we are beginning to build in this quite wretched little piece of autonomy. I think the general feeling is that it will be sandwiched between Jordan and Israel. It will be at most a corridor for Israeli businessmen who are trying to make inroads into these vast, to them untapped markets, including those of the Gulf. I can tell you that the Egyptians, for example, the Egyptian manufacturing association and bankers and others of the private sector are extremely worried about the Gaza-Jericho accord precisely because it puts their efforts and their base very much at risk by an Israeli economic penetration. The same is true of Lebanon. There's quite a churning cauldron here throughout the Middle East. I think the question of a Palestinian state at this point in the context of these remarks is just the tip of the iceberg. I don't think it's the whole story.

There's a report today quoting Nabil Shaath, who's leading the delegation at the Taba, Egypt, discussions. He said that the Palestinians had to overcome Israeli fears that they were asking for the junctions of a full-fledged independent state. He said, "The international telephone calls, the stamps, the Palestinian pound, these are all issues. In my mind they have never been exclusive for states, but the Israelis have to be convinced."

Mr. Shaath is an old friend of mine. He is a very loyal spokesperson for Mr. Arafat. It's hard for me to understand the changes in his position. He's been consistent about this all along, the last six or seven months since September. But there are different meanings to symbols. Take, for example, the idea of Palestinian currency. The Israeli position is, Yes, let them have a Palestinian currency, even a pound note with Arafat's picture on it. But it'll be like the pound notes of the Bank of Scotland. They're totally worthless, and they would be part of the Israeli monetary system. So the Israelis are perfectly capable of granting all the things that Mr. Shaath is talking about, what are referred to as symbols of sovereignty, and withholding sovereignty at the same time. That's what I'm afraid of. We've done nothing that certainly can't be done by clever negotiations. They always accept the Israeli conditions. We've done nothing to lessen the load of the occupation. We've done nothing to drive the Israelis off by organized marches, by continuing the methods of the intifada but more concentrated, more organized and more coordinated with all Palestinian resources at present. We're still a wealthy and well-endowed community. Nothing has been mobilized. We're an unmobilized people. The idea is by sitting in these talks in Taba and Paris and Washington, there are three sets going on simultaneously now, under the patronage of the U.S. and Egypt, principally, we hope by clever talking and finagling to get a good deal. But a good deal is not independence, and it's not liberation. I'm afraid Dr. Shaath has really lost sight of the main goal.

One of your epigraphs in *Orientalism* is, "They can't represent themselves. They must be represented." Has that been the case in the so-called peace process?

The tragedy is that the usefulness of the PLO or of Yasser Arafat's PLO to the whole thing is that it precisely is representative. But it's representative of Palestinians and the Palestinian people without at the same time now having either the popularity or the legitimacy or shall we say the drive and bite that it once had. This is a PLO that has been stripped of everything but its name. The fact that it has only this last shred of legitimacy is why the Israelis are carrying it along. I think there's a fundamental discrepancy between what the PLO believes about Israel's use for it and what Israel in fact intends for the PLO. It's actually quite a brilliant stroke. Over the last few years over a hundred-plus countries recognized Palestine. So the Israelis said, Let's turn that to our advantage. Here is a leadership that is totally cut off from its people. It's never been weaker. It's corrupt. Its reputation has never been worse. Let's use that international standing to our advantage. Get them to sign pretty much what we want. Then we'll see. But beyond that we don't have much use for them. I think the calculation of the PLO is based on the fact that once they've fallen in the embrace of the Israelis they're going to be kept there. I think they're wrong. I think that once the various subdeals are concluded, like the one just signed in Cairo last week, there's not going to be a use for it anymore. He will go, if he goes ever, to the town of Jericho and he'll get sunk in a situation where he has to restore law and order under the aegis and tutelage and even supervision of the Israelis, who will continue to control the borders despite the fact that there will be a Palestinian customs shed. If you look at the agreement, which I have, you will see that it's a very patronizing one and that the symbols of authority about which Dr. Shaath was talking are there, but they are meaningless. Control, power, final determination are still in the hands of the Israelis.

That was acknowledged on the front page of the *New York Times* a few days ago. They made it rather clear that Israel was the "senior partner" in the talks.

Exactly. Although Dr. Shaath again has frequently been quoted as saying from the beginning of the declaration of principles in Oslo until now there's "complete parity between the Israeli and Palestinian sides." That's a figment of his imagination, I'm afraid.

It's the parity, perhaps, of an elephant and an ant.

Right.

What are your contacts inside the West Bank and Gaza saying?

It's quite widespread. I speak to them a lot. I visit. I am visited. I have yet to meet and speak to anyone from a really quite broad range of opinion and social position who is satisfied with the status quo. I think the main fear is not only, obviously, that the Israelis got a fantastic deal, which is quite evident to anyone with a brain to use, but also that with the advent of this limited authority which the PLO is going to have, a lot of people coming in from the outside who never spent time in jail, who have been living in luxury in Europe or Tunisia, are going to come in and start to rule over people who have been fighting a battle for liberation and independence for the last twenty-seven or twenty-eight years. That's the general impression I have from the people I speak to.

The Middle East Justice Network has a newsletter called *Breaking the Siege*. It speaks, in its latest issue, of Palestinians in the occupied ter-

ritories as "a demoralized society. Apathy and despair are overwhelming sections of the community," and of, ominously, "growing armed violence which is threatening to fragment civil society."

This is the new thing. Arafat again today, February 17, in the *New York Times*, is complaining about this, that the Israelis are letting in a lot of arms to factions on the West Bank and Gaza who are wreaking havoc. The fact is that they are also giving arms to his own people. Widespread reports, again. I'm not relying on the Western media or the Israeli media, but on people on the ground who tell me that gangs now, speaking in the name of Fatah, which is the largest of the Palestinian groups, directly under Mr. Arafat's control, wander through the territories. They destroy houses. They punish people. They confiscate land. They maraud. All in the interests of a coming so-called authority.

Of course the big question in all of this is whether there will ever be any elections, and what is the meaning of elections in a situation where the street is controlled in this way by gangs. Hamas, the Islamic resistance movement, has been active, of course. Its role is quite obscure, that is to say, it's partly, of course, resisting the occupation, partly opposing the peace accord, but also setting itself up, it seems, for sharing in authority. They command an important segment of the population. They can bring people out onto the streets. So that's a second factor.

A third factor are disaffected members of the PLO who have turned against the PLO leadership in Tunis, the so-called Fatah hawks, as they're referred to, who are engaged in fights against their former comrades.

A fourth element is the various Israeli undercover units. For the first time that I've ever seen, there was an item announced in the

Israeli press where the annual Israeli budget now has a specific clause in it for these underground groups which use collaborators, have people in disguise going in to create a situation of confusion and terror. So if Arafat and his people get into Jericho, what in fact they will inherit is an unholy mess. The Israelis are very happy to have it off their hands, although at the same time they say, If anything affects our security we're going to go back in again and do what we have to.

I think it was during one of our first meetings that you told me that in telling the Palestinian story to American audiences at least you always had to start at the beginning. Is that still true?

Yes, I think so. Because I feel very strongly now, after the Oslo agreement, that the discrepancy between that wretched piece of paper and the enormous history of dispossession and suffering and loss that are in fact the story of Palestine is so great that it has to be told. It has to be narrated. It can't just disappear. I wrote a column in Arabic several weeks ago in which I said, Who is responsible for the past? The PLO certainly isn't any more. Their people at the UN, in collaboration with the Israelis, are revising some of the old UN resolutions. There is now a total willingness on the part of PLO representatives and supporters in places like Europe and the U.S. to collaborate with pro-Israeli and pro-Zionist groups under the platform of, Let's forget the past and learn how to live together. Whereas there still are 12,000 or 13,000 Palestinian prisoners who languish in Israeli jails. There are literally millions of Palestinian refugees who have had no reparation and their status is still undetermined. There are refugees existing in various countries without a status.

Third, and most important, is that the people who have suffered the ravages of occupation for the last twenty-seven or twenty-eight years, not a word has been said about their reparations. The fact is that their economy was destroyed. Their houses were blown up. Their land was taken. All of this is supposed to be, according to the current leadership of the PLO, wiped clean because a new history is about to begin. I find that totally unacceptable. Whereas in the past one felt at least that the organization representing one, the PLO, was also part of this history and was trying its best to keep that history alive and get it some realization of fulfillment in self-determination and independence, albeit minimal ones, has now joined the other side and is talking about the obliteration of the past. The idea of a collective memory is now rapidly becoming disallowed even by Palestinians. That's something which I find unacceptable. I find myself constantly remembering the numbers of people I knew, not only my own family but friends and associates and comrades, who have suffered and died in a cause which is, to a certain degree now, being put on the shelf.

As a perfect symbol for me of this, contrast the speech that Arafat gave on September 13 and the speech that Rabin gave. Mahmoud Darwish and I were talking about this. We said that the person who gave the Palestinian speech was Rabin. Arafat gave a businessman's speech in which at the end he thanked everybody, for what, it's not entirely clear. The obscenity of obliterating our history with a few platitudes the way he did, given that in the past the Palestinian speech was written by people like Darwish and others, now it's written by some businessmen who are his cohorts, is part of this betrayal of history which makes it even more imperative to tell the story again.

I also think that a lot of people, certainly it's true in the Arab world, and probably in Western Europe and the U.S., are tired of the

Palestinians. They say, Well, finally you've got what you wanted, something resembling a state. That was part of the brilliance of the staging of the ceremony, which was watched around the world. You've finally got something, so start to build your state and stop complaining.

You do a lot of public speaking. Yesterday you were in Columbus, Ohio. You're going to California next week. One of the most interesting parts of your presentations is always the questions and answers. You mix it up and engage with your audience. What are people saying when they go up to the microphone?

I think now people are asking about the fine print. There's a general sense in which the euphoria of the spectacle of last September, which can't be underestimated, has dissipated. People are now troubled by the occasional remark, the occasional scene in the media of killings or an Israeli official saying, No dates are sacred. If a Palestinian were to say that, after signing a solemn international agreement ratified in the White House, all hell would break loose. But Peres says it regularly. At the same time that he said, We want Palestinians to have their dignity, he said, There are no sacred dates. So this even minimal business of getting twenty square miles around Jericho has taken already five months and could take another five before anything happens. All of this is a mystery to people who think that the agreement in fact signaled a new stage, a new phase of relationships. And they want to know why. So on the simplest level people want to know why.

It's interesting, I don't get many comments from Israelis or Israeli supporters, more Israeli supporters than Israelis themselves. In the past I used to get the formulaic question put out by various pro-

Israeli groups who would read statements at me. In such and such a place in the Gulf Mr. Arafat said that Palestine was indivisible and we must take it all back, this sort of thing. What do you say about that? That kind of hectoring question is no longer asked. I don't get that. But what I get most of the time are questions of information. People want to know. They're very anxious also, I think it's a good sign, to connect that to other places in the world where similar depredations are taking place, South Africa and so on. I think that is a growing consciousness. But I also feel that there's a general indifference to politics on campuses.

You mentioned the hectoring at public talks that you've been subjected to. Far more serious than that, you've been the subject of death threats, picketing and all sorts of abuse, which leads me to this question: You could have had a very easy and comfortable academic life. You could have written more.

You could have worked more on your music and many other things. But you chose at some point to step outside the classroom and lecture hall into this other domain, active politics. Why did you do that?

I never really felt I had a choice. At some point after 1967 I felt that I was being claimed by it. On the most immediate level by friends, who would ask me to help, to write something, to sign something, to appear at a function and speak. I felt I couldn't say no. Then by the overwhelming dimensions that were revealed to me of what this all meant. It wasn't just a matter of my ethnic background. I didn't think it was just because I was Palestinian, because at the same time that I got involved in the Palestinian struggle, with Palestinians and others, African American and the Latin American solidarity groups in this country and the African groups and so on, one realized that the Palestinian struggle had a central role in all of this because it was about justice. It was about being able to tell the truth against extremely difficult odds, and facing a very problematic opponent who was, after all, the acknowledged victim of one of the most horrible mass exterminations of human history, but who in my opinion had now become the oppressor of another people. To be able to talk about both of those, doing justice in a certain sense to both of these experiences, was an intellectual and, I thought, a moral challenge. One thing leads to another. Given the amplification in the U.S. media of one's views, whether you consider that fortunate or unfortunate is something else, but it was a fact, I felt more and more I had no choice, I began after a while to relish it. It seemed to me important to resist and to tell the story and to constantly keep myself to standards to the best of my ability of truth and universality that I felt had to be upheld. I thought it was part of my intellectual vocation.

By the middle of the 1980s I couldn't make the distinction between a professor and an intellectual. I thought that one entailed the other. To be a professor didn't to me mean, as my mother often would try to convince me that it did, being a closeted technician who focused on one subject and did it well, but it entailed a sense of an intellectual vocation, which I found exemplified in the works and lives of other people, like Chomsky and my friend Eqbal Ahmad. So one didn't feel alone. And there were so many other Palestinians who suffered and had a much worse time than I did. I'm a creature of privilege, comparatively. So I felt that I had a responsibility to do it. There I was. I didn't really have time most of these years to think about it in quite an elaborate way as this. But that's the way I would answer it.

I'm interested in this culture of resistance and creating it, but not only resistance, because that suggests a reactive component, but something that promotes positive alternatives.

I don't think past the very early stages of surprise and consternation, when historically native peoples felt themselves beset by invasions, people coming from abroad to take their land and settle on it and do with it what they wanted. Past those early stages I think resistance always meant standing up, fighting, but also in the process positing an alternative to the present situation. It struck me as implicit in the Palestinian struggle, for example, that we from the very beginning as a movement said that we were not interested in another separatist nationalism. That's when I joined the movement. We were not interested in just another nationalism, resisting theirs in order to have ours, that we were going to be the mirror image of them. That just as they had Zionism we would have Zionism too, except it would be Palestinian. But rather that we were talking about an alternative in which the discriminations made on the basis of race and religion and national origin would be transcended by something that we called liberation. That's reflected in the name of the Palestine Liberation Organization. That, it seems to me, is the essence of resistance. It's not stubbornly putting your foot in the door, but opening a window. One of the saddest things, I believe, in the history of twentieth-century liberation movements is the betrayal of liberation by short-range goals such as independence and the establishment of a state. In the case of the Palestinians we didn't even get that far and we took a route out. I think a lot of it has to do with the absence of a general culture. I think what we relied on was a lot of slogans. We were very involved in the politics of the Arab world, which have been going since the 1950s through a downward spiral of degradation, corruption, oligarchy, dependence, and tyranny. We were affected by all that negatively, although at the beginning we were the people who spoke the most eloquently about freedom, democracy and the right to expression, the absence of censorship. But I think in the end our environment got us down.

The most important thing was a sense that you had to keep changing your goals. One thing, for example, about the ANC and Mandela, I know it's fashionable to be critical of them, but there was never any doubt in the minds of all the people who fought apartheid that the goal, the alternative to apartheid, was one person, one vote. In the case of the Palestinians that was our idea, too, from the beginning, but then we changed it. It was a secular democratic state. Then it became a state on whatever part of Palestine that could be liberated. Then it became autonomy. Then it became limited autonomy. Then it became in effect collaboration with the Israelis. So if you can't maintain a culture of resistance and alternatives, then you're going to be subject to sort of a bazaar, where alternatives are changed almost with the season. Whereas a few years ago Arafat was talking as if he was a commander of a red brigade in the early days of the Russian Revolution, he has now ended up talking as if he was a functionary in the U.S. State Department. I think that's what's been most disheartening. I would therefore say that the imperative, in my opinion, now, both in the Arab world and in the Palestinian world, more specifically, is in fact to reexamine the idea of resistance and the culture of resistance. We are now on a new stage. What the Israelis want is a normalization of relationships between Israel and the Arab states including the Palestinians. Of course I'm all for normalization. But I think real normalization can come only between equals. You have to be able to discriminate between tutelage and dependency on the one

hand and independence and standing up as a co-equal with your interlocutor. We haven't done that. That's why I think it's the most important political task for the coming decade.

**You took my question on the culture of resistance straight to Palestine
and the Middle East. I was interested in your views about the U.S.**

It's difficult to say now. The left, to which I belong, is in a state of
disarray. There is the phenomenon of post-Marxism. There's post-
colonialism. There's post-modernism. There are a lot of "posts"
around. Intellectually I think that most of them are incoherent. They
have very little to do with the social struggles and complex political
and above all economic issues which face us today. I think that's a
transformation of the landscape as such now that the American left
seems to have taken the easy alternative and has become largely academic and largely divorced from the world of intervention and the
public realm, with a few exceptions. There still are a number of public intellectuals, again like Chomsky and a few others who still persist
in trying to tell the truth. But the public realm is also full of tokenized
intellectuals who had been once perhaps symbols of resistance and
principle and have now become media figures and stars of the lecture
platform. As a result the message has become muted.

So I find, at least from the point of view of the American intellectual, the absence of a discourse of resistance, of a discourse of common principles, of common goals, social, political, economic, and of
course cultural as well, to be really disheartening. There is also in
many of the movements that were actively resistant during the
1960s, the ethnic communities, the women's movement, a kind of
parochialism, I think, which is today quite prevalent. One hopes that

it will disappear, perhaps, and that a general set of themes and concerns will appear. But it doesn't seem that's going to happen any time very soon. At this point, all that one can hope for is to stir up debate about these issues, which is what a number of us are trying to do.

Are you talking about the culture of identity?

Yes. I mean the culture of identity. I mean what Robert Hughes calls the "culture of complaint," the culture above all of special interests. I would call it the culture of professionalism. It is completely sapping a lot of the energy of movements that were active during the 1960s, the Vietnam War, and so on. The energy from them has been sapped and taken into smaller avenues. The U.S. still remains, for example, a very great power on a world scale. The effects of its power on many communities around the world needs to be assessed and criticized in a consistent way. There are very few organs today, platforms where one can speak, generally. The *Nation* is one. *Z* is another. The *Progressive* is a third. But those are just a tiny handful in a generally homogenizing intellectual landscape.

This whole issue of authentic voices and who gets to speak, for example, seems to be central to this particular debate.

I think it's become almost too central. The idea is that we have to have a representative from X community and Y community. I think at some point it can be useful. It certainly was useful to me. At a certain moment there was a felt need for an authentic Palestinian or an authentic Arab to say things, and then one could say it. But I think one has to always go beyond that, not simply accept the role but constantly challenge the format, challenge the setting, challenge the context, to expand it, to the larger issues that lurk behind these. It's not just a question of simple representation and an authentic voice. Like having a tenor, a soprano, an alto, and a bass in a chorus. But a much larger social issue which has to do with social change. That's what's lacking at the present moment.

I'm not going to ask you the ritualistic final question; which is, What projects are you working on? But a lot of people are concerned about your health. They ask me about you. What can you tell them?

It's a holding pattern. I have a chronic disease, leukemia. It has its bad moments. You get secondary effects which can be treated. I had one last fall. It was treated successfully. Now I'm OK. I try not to think about the future too much. One has to just keep going. But in general I feel much better about myself and my situation and my health.

They're synonymous with each other. I think the big battle is to try to not make it the center of your every waking moment, put it aside and press on with the tasks at hand. I've got a lot to say and write, I feel, and I just want to go on doing that.

INDEX

ABOUT THE CONTRIBUTORS

Eqbal Ahmad was Professor of Politics at Hampshire College in western Massachusetts. A Fellow of the Institute for Policy Studies, he lectured and published widely on Middle East and Third World issues. He served as joint editor of the British journal *Race & Class*.

Dr. Nubar Hovsepian is Associate Professor of Political Science and International Studies and is the Academic Director of the MA program in International Studies at Chapman University. He holds a PhD in Political Science from the Graduate Center—City University of New York. He edited *The War on Lebanon* (2007). His new book, *Palestinian State Formation: Education and the Construction of National Identity*, was published in 2008. He is currently working on a book on Edward Said as a public intellectual. In addition, he has written and edited four books (in Arabic), most notably on the Iranian revolution of 1979. He served as Political Affairs officer at the United Nations (1982–84), and has worked as publisher, journalist, and development specialist.

David Barsamian is the award-winning founder and director of Alternative Radio based in Boulder, Colorado (www.alternativeradio.org). He is the author of numerous books with Noam Chomsky, Howard Zinn, Eqbal Ahmad, Tariq Ali, and Arundhati Roy. His latest book is *Targeting Iran*. In December 2007, he gave the Eqbal Ahmad lectures in Karachi, Islamabad, and Lahore.

Edward W. Said was University Professor of English and Comparative Literature at Columbia. He was born in Jerusalem, Palestine, in 1935. He attended schools there and in Cairo. He did his undergraduate work at Princeton and earned his graduate degree at Harvard. A prolific writer, he is the author of *Orientalism, The Question of Palestine, Covering Islam, After the Last Sky, Culture and Imperialism, The Politics of Dispossession, Representations of the Intellectual,* and many other books and articles.

ALSO FROM HAYMARKET BOOKS

A Little Piece of Ground
Elizabeth Laird • Life in occupied Palestine, through the eyes of a young boy. Winner: Middle East Outreach Council Youth Literature Award, 2006, and the U.S. Board on Books for Young People's Outstanding International Book Award, 2007. • ISBN 9781931859387

Between the Lines:
Readings on Israel, the Palestinians, and the U.S. "War on Terror"
Tikva Honig-Parnass and Toufic Haddad • This compilation of essays, edited by a Palestinian writer and an Israeli journalist, constitutes a challenge to critically rethink the Israeli-Palestinian conflict. • ISBN 9781931859448

Beyond the Green Zone:
Dispatches from an Unembedded Journalist in Occupied Iraq
Dahr Jamail • Jamail's critically acclaimed, indispensable account of life in Iraq under U.S. occupation, now available in paperback, with a new afterword. This widely read account offers lyrical journalism, personal reflection, incisive analysis, and groundbreaking reportage, including previously unpublished details of the first years of occupation. • ISBN 9781931859615

Blackwater: El Auge del Ejercito Mercenario Mas Poderoso del Mundo
Jeremy Scahill • The *New York Times* bestselling exposé, in a fully revised and updated paperback edition, in Spanish. • ISBN 9781931859622

Breaking the Sound Barrier
Amy Goodman, edited by Denis Moynihan • Amy Goodman, award-winning host of the daily, internationally broadcast radio and television program *Democracy Now!*, breaks through the corporate media's lies, sound bites, and silence in this wide-ranging new collection of articles. • ISBN 9781931859998

Civil Rights in Peril
Edited by Elaine C. Hagopian • Winner: Myers Outstanding Book Award, 2004, from the Gustavus Myers Center. Muslims and Arab Americans are in-

creasingly under attack as a result of the U.S. "war on terror"—at home, as well as abroad. *Civil Rights in Peril* explores the impact on Muslims and Arabs, and shows how ordinary people can resist these attacks on our fundamental rights. • ISBN 9780745322650

Class Struggle and Resistance in Africa
Edited by Leo Zeilig • Employing Marxist theory to address the postcolonial problems of several different countries, experts analyze such issues as the renewal of Islamic fundamentalism in Egypt, debt relief, trade union movements, and strike action. Includes interviews with leading African socialists and activists. • ISBN 9781931859684

Diary of Bergen Belsen: 1944–45
Hanna Lévy-Hass, foreword and afterword by Amira Hass • Hanna Lévy-Hass stands alone as the only resistance fighter to record her own experience inside the camps, and she does so with unflinching clarity and attention to the political and social divisions inside Bergen Belsen. • ISBN 9781931859875

Essays
Wallace Shawn • In these beautiful essays acclaimed playwright and actor Wallace Shawn takes readers on a revelatory journey through high art, war, politics, culture, and privilege. • ISBN 9781608460021

Field Notes on Democracy: Listening to Grasshoppers
Arundhati Roy • Combining fierce conviction, deft political analysis, and beautiful writing, this essential new book from Arundhati Roy examines the dark side of democracy in contemporary India. Roy looks closely at how religious majoritarianism, cultural nationalism, and neofascism simmer just under the surface of a country that projects itself as the world's largest democracy. • ISBN 9781608460243

Hopes and Prospects
Noam Chomsky • The Americas, both North and South, have been in motion with elections and political shifts that Noam Chomsky explores here with his characteristic independence and insight. • ISBN 9781931859967

Notes from the Middle World

Breyten Breytenbach • Internationally distinguished South African artist, activist, and writer Breyten Breytenbach delivers a new collection of essays that traces the collisions between utopia and disaster, political trauma, and the renewal of hope. • ISBN 9781931859912

Poetry and Protest: A Dennis Brutus Reader

Dennis Brutus, edited by Aisha Karim and Lee Sustar • This vital original collection of interviews, poetry, and essays of the much-loved anti-apartheid leader is the first book of its kind to bring together the full, forceful range of his work. • ISBN 9781931859226

The Meek and the Militant: Religion and Power Across the World

Paul N. Siegel • This reprint of a Marxist classic sheds much-needed light on the impact of religion on politics. *The Meek and the Militant* examines the historical roots of religion around the world, its origin and persistence, and how it has acted as a bulwark of the social order and also as a revolutionary force. • ISBN 9781931859240

The Struggle for Palestine

Edited by Lance Selfa • *The Struggle for Palestine* gets behind the headlines and myths about the occupation and the "peace process" to expose the role of the U.S. government in sponsoring Israel's war against the Palestinians. It documents the efforts of Palestinians to win their freedom, and it presents a clear vision of a real solution: the creation of a secular, democratic state in all of Palestine. • ISBN 9781931859004

War Without End: The Iraq War in Context

Michael Schwartz • In this razor-sharp analysis, TomDispatch.com commentator Michael Schwartz demolishes the myths used to sell the U.S. public the idea of an endless "war on terror" centered in Iraq. In a popular style, reminiscent of the best writing against the Vietnam War, he shows how the real U.S. interests in Iraq have been rooted in the geopolitics of oil and the expansion of a neoliberal economic model in the Middle East. • ISBN 9781931859547

ABOUT HAYMARKET BOOKS

Haymarket Books is a nonprofit, progressive book distributor and publisher, a project of the Center for Economic Research and Social Change. We believe that activists need to take ideas, history, and politics into the many struggles for social justice today. Learning the lessons of past victories, as well as defeats, can arm a new generation of fighters for a better world. As Karl Marx said, "The philosophers have merely interpreted the world; the point, however, is to change it."

We take inspiration and courage from our namesakes, the Haymarket Martyrs, who gave their lives fighting for a better world. Their 1886 struggle for the eight-hour day, which gave us May Day, the international workers' holiday, reminds workers around the world that ordinary people can organize and struggle for their own liberation. These struggles continue today across the globe—struggles against oppression, exploitation, hunger, and poverty.

It was August Spies, one of the Martyrs targeted for being an immigrant and an anarchist, who predicted the battles being fought to this day. "If you think that by hanging us you can stamp out the labor movement," Spies told the judge, "then hang us. Here you will tread upon a spark, but here, and there, and behind you, and in front of you, and everywhere, the flames will blaze up. It is a subterranean fire. You cannot put it out. The ground is on fire upon which you stand."

We could not succeed in our publishing efforts without the generous financial support of our readers. Many people contribute to our project through the Haymarket Sustainers program, where donors receive free books in return for their monetary support. If you would like to be a part of this program, please contact us at info@haymarketbooks.org.

Shop our full catalog online at www.haymarketbooks.org or call 773-583-7884.

Printed in the USA
CPSIA information can be obtained
at www.ICGtesting.com
JSHW022344140824
68134JS00019B/1681

9 781931 859950